Language and Education

Papers from the
Annual Meeting of the British Association for Applied Linguistics
held at the University of Southampton, September 1995

Edited by

George M. Blue and Rosamond Mitchell

BRITISH ASSOCIATION FOR APPLIED LINGUISTICS

in association with

MULTILINGUAL MATTERS LTD
Clevedon • Philadelphia • Adelaide

Library of Congress Cataloging in Publication Data

British Association for Applied Linguistics. Meeting (25th: 1995: University of Southampton)
Language and Education: Papers from the Annual Meeting of the British Association for Applied Linguistics held at the University of Southampton, September 1995/Edited by George M. Blue and Rosamond Mitchell.
Includes bibliographical references.
1. Language and education–Congresses. I. Blue, George M. II. Mitchell, Rosamond. III. Title.
P40.8.B75   1995
418-dc20   96-31897

British Library Cataloguing in Publication Data

A CIP catalogue record for this book is available from the British Library.

ISBN 1-85359-370-2 (pbk)

Multilingual Matters Ltd

UK: Frankfurt Lodge, Clevedon Hall, Victoria Road, Clevedon BS21 7SJ.
USA: 1900 Frost Road, Suite 101, Bristol, PA 19007, USA.
Canada: OISE, 712 Gordon Baker Road, Toronto, Ontario, Canada M2H 3RT.
Australia: P.O. Box 6025, 95 Gilles Street, Adelaide, SA 5000, Australia.
South Africa: PO Box 1080, Northcliffe 2115, Johannesburg, South Africa.

Typeset by Wayside Books, Clevedon.
Printed and bound in Great Britain by the Longdunn Press.

Contents

Language and Education: Editors' preface

GEORGE M. BLUE and ROSAMOND MITCHELL
University of Southampton

The 28th Annual Meeting of BAAL was held at the Centre for Language in Education, University of Southampton in September 1995. The theme of the meeting was 'Language and Education', and over 100 papers were given. This collection therefore represents only a small sample of the wide range of applied linguistic work presented at the Meeting, connected to this theme.

In the early days of BAAL it was probably the case that nearly all the work that members were involved in would have fitted quite comfortably under the 'Language and Education' umbrella. The themes of recent Annual Meetings (e.g. 'Language and Nation', 'Language and Culture', 'Language and Change') indicate that this is no longer the case. Similarly, in the early days of BAAL it could have safely been assumed that the kind of education that members were involved in was for the most part foreign language teaching. Although this remains an important strand within the association, the present collection shows that applied linguists now share many different concerns within the educational field as well as outside it.

In planning the 1995 Annual Meeting we divided the major theme area into three sub-themes: 'Mother Tongue Classrooms', 'Second/Foreign Language Classrooms' and 'Language Policy and Education'. Although all of the papers selected for publication could be related to one or more of these headings, when we came to the publication this no longer seemed to be the most logical way of dividing up this particular set of papers. Three of the four plenary papers address 'Educational/Applied Linguistics Discourses', and we have grouped them together under this heading. Two papers (including the fourth plenary) deal with 'Language Policy and Education'; so we have kept this sub-theme. A further two papers could be seen as dealing with aspects of 'Professional Culture' and the final batch of three with 'Learner Language in Educational Settings'. Although we do not wish to suggest any watertight or rigid compartmentalisation, we shall present the papers in this order, under these four headings.

Educational/Applied Linguistics Discourses

Christopher Brumfit's plenary paper (the Pit Corder lecture) is a wide-ranging review of Applied Linguistics, how it has developed as a field, how it is conceived of today, and its relationship with Educational Linguistics. It ends with a discussion of the positivist-relativist tension, a theme which is thoroughly developed by Jim Lantolf in the next paper. Lantolf suggests that in a field so full of controversy as second language acquisition, the post-modernist position may be an appropriate response to a bewildering variety of conflicting theories. Finally in this section Neil Mercer looks at the role of language within the learning/teaching process, in particular 'the ways language is used as a social mode of thinking, and for guiding the construction of knowledge'.

Language Policy and Education

Jenny Cheshire's plenary contrasts issues of language policy and practice in education in largely monolingual England with multilingual Switzerland, arguing that applied linguists need to engage with these issues in order to influence policy decisions. Tom Bloor and Wondwosen Tamrat offer a case study of issues of language policy (mainly though not exclusively in education) in multilingual Ethiopia, and evaluate the impact of present policy changes for the respective roles of English and Amharic.

Professional Culture in Language Education

Alan Davies is interested in the role of theory in language testing, and he investigates the extent to which language testing practice is really influenced by current theoretical frameworks of communicative language ability. In a quite different area of professional culture, Simon Gieve investigates and questions the theoretical and philosophical assumptions that lie behind attempts to inculturate international students (in this case, Malaysian teachers) into British academic culture.

Learner Language in Educational Settings

Tony Cowie and Peter Howarth's paper deals with both international and British students and compares their ability to use so-called 'restricted collocations' in their writing. Alison Wray turns her attention to British undergraduates and investigates a number of common errors in their written English, with some pedagogic implications. Finally, Gee Macrory and Valerie Stone's paper focuses on British school pupils and looks at both their knowledge of and their ability to use the present perfect form in French.

Thus, despite the limitations of length, it will be seen that this collection gives at least a flavour of the breadth and variety of applied linguistic activity in the field of 'Language and Education'. Moreover, the fact that the papers cannot be easily pigeonholed does, we believe, illustrate something of the rich inter-relationships that exist within the field.

1 Educational Linguistics, Applied Linguistics and the Study of Language Practices[1]

University of Southampton

Introduction: the Scope of Applied Linguistics

Pit Corder in discussion once remarked that educational practice demands 'implied linguistics' rather than applied linguistics. In this paper I wish to show how many underlying concerns about the implications of linguistics for our work are perennial, particularly those about the relationship with language in education.

BAAL's Constitution, originally adopted in 1967, reads: 'The Objects of the Association are ... the study of language use, language acquisition and language teaching, and the fostering of inter-disciplinary collaboration in this study...' Until recently the Association's headed paper used its name against a backdrop of listed areas of study: 'language acquisition, language teaching, language disabilities, language varieties, language in literature, language policies, languages in social services, translation, interpretation'. Yet against this apparently imperialistic claim on many fields we have to set the tendency for other bodies to be formed to develop their own specialisms. Associations for teachers of particular languages already existed when BAAL was set up with Pit Corder as its distinguished first Chair, but since then students of Second Language Acquisition, Poetics and Linguistics, Lexicography, French Language Studies, Language Awareness and no doubt other fields have established their own associations, operating simultaneously as rivals and collaborators with BAAL. With the theme of this 28th Annual Meeting 'Language and Education', it is interesting to note that (despite longstanding claims for 'Educational

Linguistics', e.g. Spolsky, 1978; Stubbs, 1986) there is no separate British association for educational language work, while CLIE (the Committee for Linguistics in Education) arose from joint meetings between BAAL and LAGB, and is under the joint control of the two associations. Its substantive function is 'to explore and evaluate ways in which linguistics and applied linguistics might contribute towards the school curriculum and the professional training of teachers' (1980 terms of reference, revised 1984), and it has produced a succession of valuable pamphlets to this end.

Nonetheless, we could ask of Applied Linguistics, as J. D. Palmer did in Kaplan's 1977 symposium: 'Should we not discard the name? Let's call it language teaching, or stylistics, or dialectology, or phonology, or syntactic theory, or whatever it is' (1980: 26).

The purpose of this paper is not to defend separate associations for linguists, language teachers or others. Indeed, one of BAAL's major justifications is, as the preamble to the Membership List makes clear, 'to provide a common forum for those engaged in the theoretical study of language and for those whose interest is in the practical implications of such work'. Nonetheless, the very broad conceptualisation of its role that BAAL has adopted requires some defence, for it is not vulnerable simply to the charge of academic imperialism; it could be charged with vagueness, incoherence and confusion. Members could be regarded as those who are left over when the serious or technically-minded have identified themselves elsewhere; alternatively, this could be the forum in which theoreticians and researchers with a social conscience (including but not exclusively linguists) explain themselves to atheoretical practitioners; or as the forum in which 'performance', 'language in use', 'linguistic social practices' and similar themes are explored and studied. All of these views are represented in discussion (though the first is too offensive to appear in writing), and no doubt some elements of BAAL's activity could be related to all of these, even the offensive one. But they are, in my view, inadequate accounts of an appropriate rationale for a discipline/field/subject such as Applied Linguistics. There is a much stronger case to be made, which is more abstract than those referred to above, but defensible (indeed I shall argue essential) for the well-being of our understanding of language, human beings and education.

Applied Linguistics as Mediation

It is curious, when we have all recognised from Saussure the arbitrariness of the sign, how difficult we find it to free ourselves from the centrality of Linguistics to Applied Linguistics, even when the function and practices of the association may have shifted. Yet decisions have to be made that reflect social structures (such as departments within higher education), and most would agree that Applied Linguistics makes more sense with Linguistics in the Research Assessment Exercise than with any of the single, and equally arbitrary, sub-areas within which most BAAL members work. Nonetheless, in this as in other ways, it suffers from all the problems of inter-disciplinary areas, and all the problems of applied areas. Might it not be better, therefore, to accept a straight 'Linguistics Applied' perspective, to use Widdowson's formulation from BAAL's 1979 Annual Meeting (Widdowson, 1980: 165), and follow the precepts of our founding fathers? If not that, might it be better to argue that we are the repository of what another former Chair, Sam Spicer, called 'real understanding of real language', and to concentrate on the strong model of 'language in use'? Either of these would make our self-definition tidier – but I hope to show that either would also weaken the value of our work and result in lower quality research and theorising than an alternative definition of applied linguistics, namely 'the theoretical and empirical investigation of real-world problems in which language is a central issue' (Brumfit, 1995b: 27).

Much discussion of what Applied Linguistics is relates to parallel debates about what Linguistics is. The distinction between linguistic and applied linguistic scholarship is of course very old, for classical rhetorical studies were clearly applied in intention. Robins (1967: 13) implies that linguistic scholarship in Plato and Aristotle relates merely to the skill of reading and writing, but Plato's Philebus shows Socrates clearly concerned with meta-classification:

> The unlimited variety of sound was once discerned by some god, or perhaps some godlike man; you know the story that there was some such person in Egypt called Theuth. He it was who originally discerned the existence, in that unlimited variety, of the vowels – not 'vowel' in the singular but 'vowels' in the plural ... (Hamilton & Cairns, 1961: 1094; Hackforth's translation)

And the classification continues, with considerable subtlety.

It is harder to find meta-statements (as distinct from exemplifications) on the distinction between theoretical and applied language study. The eminent Danish linguist Rasmus Rask (1787–1832) is cited (Gregersen, 1991: 12) as distinguishing between theoretical linguistics (discovering and formulating laws) and applied (explanations of words and grammar). But Howatt (1984: 265) dates the term 'Applied Linguistics' to the launch of *Language Learning – a Quarterly Journal of Applied Linguistics* in 1948.

For practical purposes, though, we should start when discussion of the nature of Applied Linguistics proliferated in the 1960s and 1970s, as the national and international associations, including BAAL, were founded.

A seminal book, *The Linguistic Sciences and Language Teaching* (Halliday, McIntosh & Strevens, 1964: 138), comments, 'applied linguistics starts when a description is specifically made, or an existing description used, for a further purpose which lies outside the linguistic sciences'.

Such early discussions were confident about the relationship between linguistics and applied areas like language teaching, though they anticipated many of the difficulties that are still raised about any simple relationship between linguistics and practice. Mackey expressed the problems with exemplary clarity. His complete definition/historical note in 1966 was:

What is applied linguistics?

The term 'applied linguistics' seems to have originated in the United States in the 1940s. It was first used by persons with an obvious desire to be identified as scientists rather than as humanists; the association with 'applied science' can hardly have been accidental. Yet, although linguistics is a science, 'applied science' does not necessarily include linguistics.

The creation of applied linguistics as a discipline represents an attempt to find practical applications for 'modern scientific linguistics'. While assuming that linguistics can be an applied science, it brings together such diverse activities as the making of alphabets by missionaries and the making of translations by machines. The use of the term has now become crystallized in the names of language centres, reviews, books, and articles. (Mackey, 1966: 247)

But he raises several substantive difficulties:

Contemporary claims that applied linguistics can solve all the problems of language teaching are as unfounded as the claims that applied psychology can solve them. For the problems of language teaching are central neither to psychology nor linguistics. Neither science is equipped to solve the problems of language teaching.

It is likely that language teaching will continue to be a child of fashion in linguistics and psychology until the time it becomes an autonomous discipline which uses these related sciences instead of being used by them. To become autonomous it will, like any science, have to weave its own net, so as to fish out from the oceans of human experience and natural phenomena only the elements it needs ... (1966: 255)

Politzer (1972: 2) posits a fictional teacher, 'Mr Jones', to make his position clear:

Mr Jones has utilized linguistics or has had recourse to *Applied Linguistics* in the sense in which the term is used in this publication, because Mr Jones has gone through the following process:

(1) He has recognised a pedagogical problem.

(2) He has utilized his knowledge of linguistics to formulate an assumption concerning the precise nature of the pedagogical problem.

(3) He has utilized his knowledge of linguistics to formulate another assumption concerning a way of dealing with the pedagogical problem.

(4) He has devised teaching procedures based on this assumption and has tested it, at least in a very informal sort of way.

But he also refers to other areas (sociolinguistics, psycholinguistics), and other disciplines (psychology of learning, social psychology) in formulating the 'conclusion concerning teaching procedures' (pp. 2–3). He reflects the psychologism of the period in asserting boldly 'Applied linguistics may be considered as a branch of psycholinguistics' (p. 2), and he recognises that linguistics could be applied to areas other than language teaching.

The Politzer formulation suggests a technology drawing upon linguistics which is less humane and educationally sensitive than Mackey's. A year later, Pit Corder extends this notion to one of theoretical dependence:

The application of linguistic knowledge to some object – or applied linguistics, as its name implies – is an activity. It is not a theoretical study. It makes use of the findings of theoretical studies. The applied linguist is a consumer, or user, not a producer, of theories ... Language teaching is also an activity, but teaching languages is not the same activity as applied linguistics. (Corder, 1973: 10)

Thus by the mid-1970s the notion of Applied Linguistics, albeit limited to language teaching, was both marketable, and – by implication – unproblematic. For example, Wardhaugh (1974) allows us to interpret Applied Linguistics inductively by using the title *Topics in Applied Linguistics* for a book, but not making any definition; instead he concentrates on items of linguistically informed commentary on (e.g.) spelling, reading, and second language teaching.

A definition deriving from Corder is still commonplace in basic dictionaries and reference books:

Crystal, in *A First Dictionary of Linguistics and Phonetics* (1980):

A branch of linguistics where the primary concern is the application of linguistic theories, methods and findings to the elucidation of language problems which have arisen in other areas of experience. (1980: 28–9)

(repeated with minimal modification in Crystal, *The Cambridge Encyclopedia of Language,* 1987: 412)

Richards *et al., Longman Dictionary of Applied Linguistics* (1985):

(1) the study of second and foreign language learning and teaching.

(2) the study of language and linguistics in relation to practical problems, such as LEXICOGRAPHY, TRANSLATION, SPEECH PATHOLOGY, etc. .... (p. 15, and again in the second edition, 1992, retitled *The Longman Dictionary of Language Teaching and Applied Linguistics,* p. 19)

Kaplan and Widdowson in the *International Encyclopedia of Linguistics* (Bright, 1992: 76):

a technology which makes abstract ideas and research findings accessible and relevant to the real world; it mediates between theory and practice.

Thus there seemed to be, as Buckingham & Eskey (1980) indicate in a 1977 TESOL symposium that preceded the setting up of the American Association of Applied Linguistics, 'general agreement that ... applied linguists perform a *mediating* function between theoretical disciplines and various kinds of more practical work' (p. 2). However, the debate does not stop there, and even applied linguists who have drafted these definitions, such as Crystal and Widdowson, may, as we shall see, move beyond mediation in their practice. Buckingham and Eskey, indeed, go on to suggest that Linguistics is reconnected with real world language by Applied Linguistics. Others in the same symposium follow Krashen (1980) in accepting a limited and top-down model. For him, Applied Linguistics is concerned with 'the creation of materials and methods for second language teaching. Research in applied linguistics consists of comparisons of materials and methods, with student progress in L2 performance as the dependent variable ...' (p. 13).

Applied Linguistics as an (Inter-)Discipline

However, another strand of argument was visible. BAAL's second Chair, Peter Strevens, had already, in a memo for AILA 1975 (published as Strevens, 1980), pressed Corder's definition further. Applied Linguistics involved both theory and practice, had multiple bases, not just Linguistics, and was broader than language learning and teaching alone. Most interestingly, he observed that it 'redefines itself afresh for each task' (p. 19), and is dynamic, not static. This account is distinguished from others by its sensitivity to context and awareness of the richness of potential source material.

Other linguists were also expressing doubts about the Linguistics Applied model. Spolsky made a clear statement of the case in 1978:

> ... the structural linguists applied their efforts to replace a system based on one limited view of language (the translation method) by an equally rigid and psycholinguistically invalid approach (the audio-lingual method). When this system turned out to be inadequate, there were many who thought that all that was needed was to come up with a new one based on the latest theory of language. (Spolsky, 1978: 2)

His solution is to propose an 'Educational Linguistics' in order to escape a perceived closer link to Linguistics rather than to (e.g.) pedagogy.

However, building on hints in Strevens' paper, this position was superseded by a more ambitious programme. Widdowson, introducing *Explorations in Applied Linguistics* (1979: 1), still works within the Language Teaching model, but makes grander and more holistic claims:

> Applied linguistics, as I conceive it, is a spectrum of inquiry which extends from theoretical studies of language to classroom practice. The papers appearing here explore issues that can be located at different points on this spectrum: some with a focus on matters of a predominantly theoretical kind, others with a primary focus on matters of practical pedagogy. But in all cases the whole spectrum is presupposed as the context of discussion ...

Furthermore, Corder's avoidance of theoretical concern is explicitly repudiated:

> Language teaching is necessarily a theoretical as well as a practical occupation. If this were not so, discussion on the matter would reduce to an exchange of anecdotes and pedagogy would be a mere pretence ... A communicative orientation involves a consideration of a whole host of issues: – how discourse is processed, how interaction is conducted, learning styles and strategies, developmental patterns of language acquisition, the role of learner and teacher – all these and more. (pp. 2–3)

Even more grandly, Kaplan (1980: 63) notes 'I would contend that there is virtually no human activity in which the applied linguist cannot play a role'. Certainly many British linguists had already engaged in an impressive variety of applied activity. Lyons' and Halliday's work on stylistics and the latter's on educational linguistics, Sinclair's on that and on lexicography, Crystal on language disability, Trim and Stubbs on teaching modern languages and English as a mother tongue respectively may all be mentioned, to restrict the list to those who started primarily as linguists rather than (as most British applied linguists did) as teachers or other practitioners.

In a book that directly arises out of an invitation to address BAAL, Crystal (1981: 2) writes: '... what one is applying is not so much knowledge about language, as a way of investigating language – a methodological, as distinct from an empirical, dimension for the subject'.

We already have, then, Applied Linguistics as a mediation, as an interdisciplinary interaction, as a technology, as a methodology, and as an autonomous theoretical and practical discipline. We could see this diversity of definition as evidence that the discipline was alive and active. In practice, though, Stern's diagram (1983: 181) is typical, treating Applied Linguistics as a technology:

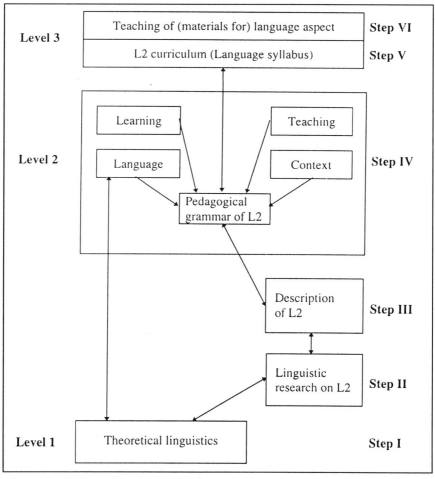

Figure 1 The interaction between linguistics and language teaching (reproduced from Stern (1983), by permission)

But it is important to point out that accounts like this are only metaphors. The psychological processes of teachers, materials writers, and curriculum designers may reflect the categories of such models, but only as integrated and largely unconscious decision-making processes; the algorithm metaphor, which underlies such boxes and arrows, does not reflect an ordered series of discrete events. Furthermore, there are completely alternative accounts possible. Reflecting on my experience of writing ESL materials in Tanzania in the late 1960s, I could have modified Stern's categories with some justice, reading upwards on his diagram, with:

Step I: Ethics/political theory

Step II: Political theory in Tanzania

Step III: Description of sociopolitical context

Step IV: Subject matter choices/Language/Learning/Teaching

Step V: (as in Stern) L2 curriculum

Step VI: (as in Stern) Teaching materials

This is not to say that linguistics was ignored, nor that we lacked explicit language learning principles; only that the model above is a closer representation of our thinking in workshops in which nation-building and justice were the uppermost thoughts in our planning processes. Were we engaged in practical applications of applied linguistic theory? I had certainly been strongly influenced by Halliday, McIntosh & Strevens (1964) as a serious analysis of practical problems that I was facing daily in the classroom. But I was not in Tanzania because of teaching techniques, however principled, any more than language users habitually speak to display their syntactic skills. I was there because I believed in the Tanzanian government and wanted to create something good out of the remains of the dying British Empire. And similar motives drove many of my most professionally committed language-teaching colleagues.

You do not have to agree with these ambitions to recognise that motives are at least as important as linguistic applications in defining how we address practical problems in which language is a central issue.

Widdowson comments on the fictionality (in all sciences) of generalised statements, and remarks about application:

> You do not *apply* a theory which is a fiction, any more than you apply a novel. What you do is develop your awareness of what a useful model of behaviour might be for your particular purposes. (Widdowson, 1980: 168)

He then goes on to clarify the interrelationship between Linguistics itself and Applied Linguistics by suggesting that

> Linguistics applied works in one direction and yields descriptions which are projections of linguistic theory which exploit the data of actual language as illustration. Applied linguistics ... works in the opposite way and yields descriptions which are projections of actual language which exploit linguistic theory as illumination. (p. 169)

This is a far cry from a mediating role. It implies a sophisticated technology of its own for Applied Linguistics. Crystal, too, moves beyond mediation, commenting (1981: 18) that 'implicit in the applied linguistics enterprise is a comparative dimension'.

Thus Applied Linguistics is emerging as an integrated discipline, feeding in to Linguistics technically sophisticated statements about language in genuine social situations, on the one hand, and responding to the needs of practitioners, on the other. Carter (1990: 17) has characterised the needs of practitioners, from the point of view of outsiders, whether politicians, the press or linguists:

> ... if teachers have no formal training in linguistic awareness then they will lack categories and frameworks for thinking about and analysing crucial elements in learning and will therefore draw such categories from a common store of half-belief in which prejudice and fact combine indistinguishably.

And at least some practitioners accept such views, if Crystal (1981: 8) is correct in his assertion that 'Many professionals will listen to linguists because of "the ubiquity of failure".' Certainly, there has been a widespread hope that linguistics might resolve some problems of 'failure'. Indeed, notwithstanding the suspicion of English mother tongue teachers towards Linguistics, innovations like A-Level English Language, the LINC programme, and movements for Language Awareness and KAL (Knowledge about Language) have shown an increasing demand for greater understanding of language in the teaching of English as a mother tongue. It is noticeable, for example, that there are many more references to Linguistics in Brindley's (1994) Open University reader for training future English teachers than in its sibling, Swarbrick's (1994) book on modern languages. This would not have been the case ten years ago, and research carried out in the 1990s in Hampshire (Mitchell *et al.*, 1994) shows that the practices of experienced modern language teachers reflect the detail of linguistic analysis far more than similar English teachers' practices do.

Whatever the demand is, though, the richness of possible interpretation of linguistic data remains daunting, as Cook & Seidlhofer (1995: 4) indicate:

> Language is viewed in various theories as a genetic inheritance, a mathematical system, a social fact, the expression of individual identity, the expression of cultural identity, the outcome of dialogic interaction, a social semiotic, the intuitions of native speakers, the sum of attested data, a

collection of memorized chunks, a rule-governed discrete combinatory system, or electrical activation in a distributed network ... We do not have to choose. Language can be all of these things at once.

Because so many scholars address linguistic matters from so many perspectives, the privileging of Linguistics in Applied Linguistics is bound to attract criticism. Certainly, the claim has some force that close-to-Linguistics work is dominant in international research traditions. The rise of SLA empirical work, for example, dominated the journal *Applied Linguistics* in the late 1980s (19 out of 42 papers in volumes 8 and 9, with several of BAAL's 'areas' scarcely receiving any attention at all). But the 1990s have seen a more ferocious counter-argument developing, with a stronger underpinning in non-linguistic theory. Phillipson (1992), indicting Applied Linguistics along with other agents of 'English linguisticism', worries about the limitation to linguistics (e.g. pp. 175–6) and at the same time calls for a 'critical' applied linguistics (p. 321). Similarly, Pennycook (1994: 299) writes

One of the problems with applied linguistics ... has been its divorce from educational theory and the tendency to deal with language teaching as a predominantly psycholinguistic phenomenon isolated from its social, cultural and educational contexts.

Further, if the journal *Applied Linguistics* is typical, the concentration on first world scholarship (32 out of 40 authors from Europe or North America in volumes 8 and 9; 34 out of 45 in volumes 12 and 13, for example) suggests a heavy emphasis away from many centres of real-world practice. So Pennycook can justifiably claim that

With the gradual consolidation of applied linguistics, furthermore, there has been a constant move towards educational expertise being defined as in the hands of the predominantly male Western applied linguistic academy, rather than in the hands of the largely female teaching practitioners ... [This leads him to assert] ... we need a reconceptualization of the role of teachers and applied linguists that does away with the theory/practice divide and views teachers/applied linguists as politically engaged critical educators. (p. 303)

But while this call is close to those which are made to other theorists of practice (in Education, Medicine, and Law, for example), it needs to be treated with caution.

Language and Education

Proponents of 'Educational Linguistics', by analogy with Educational Psychology, etc., base their argument, as we have seen, on the disciplines outside

Linguistics that are relevant to language teaching. However, such an argument is relevant to *any* study of language in real world situations, and is not peculiar to Education. Further, there are many ways in which language interacts with educational activity. Apart from the direct teaching of languages (first, second or foreign), language is a crucial mediating force in processes of learning (or arguably often *is* the process of learning, if we accept the notion that learning is substantially another term for entering a new discourse community), and is a major element in establishing the school itself as an institution. Thus 'school language policies' rightly embrace the linguistic practices of teachers and administrative staff, as well as students, include language outside as well as inside the classroom, and ultimately need to relate to a conception of the role of language in the world, and hence the whole social philosophy that the school is an agent in promoting.

To separate these activities from sociological, philosophical, political, economic and psychological factors would be manifestly impossible, and once Educational Linguistics departed from Linguistics proper, there would be no point at which the list of relevant further disciplines could be stopped. Yet the arguments for not stopping at Linguistics are so overwhelming that there is little point in rehearsing them here, as they are now so universally accepted.

So in Education, as in any other social practice to which language is centrally important, the floodgates are open. Whether we like it or not, we have to learn to swim.

The Positivist–Relativist Tension

One solution that is widely proposed is to identify Linguistics with the positivist tradition that has allegedly inhibited previous discussion, and to embrace alternative philosophies, to accept the post-modernist critique, and to deny the validity of previous procedures.

Post-modernist critiques are in many respects liberating. We can, for example, accept that we each stand at the intersection of many discourses, that a single grand scheme is neither necessary nor attainable, and relax in our interdisciplinarity. But to do this we have to accept a cautious rather than a confident post-modernist position. As I have tried to show elsewhere (Brumfit, 1995a), strong emancipatory arguments about language practice, such as Tollefson's (1991: 211) identification of language with race and gender, risk allocating individuals to language groups without their consent and failing to allow the possibility of choice of linguistic repertoire. Further, a commitment to education is incompatible with a commitment to strong forms of relativism or to identification of knowledge with power. Yet all these positions may – in a weak form – highlight deficiencies in current theory and practice. Recognising processes of social construction in knowledge formation, or acknowledging implicit discrimination against particular groups are valuable services. But moving to absolute and exclusive statements that conflict with either logic or experience only feeds politicians who like convenient simplifications. In general, in human sciences, a working axiom should be the claim that 'all strong versions of argument are always wrong', because human behaviour is never consistent enough and never simple enough to be neatly encapsulated in strong versions of argument.

Total rejection of previous practice is always false to experience and to practice *because* it is total. To act on slogans, which is what strong versions do, is to fail to recognise our social and historical inter-connectedness. We are culturally different at the same time as we are culturally the same. Emphasising either to the exclusion of the other obscures the serious question, which is 'What is the relevant relationship between similarity and difference?' Philosophies which deny any universality conflict so strongly with basic experiential evidence that it is difficult to understand how they can be advanced, except for point-scoring. If we hold them consistently, we can neither allow successful individual communication, because that presumes a degree of shared experience, nor trans-ferability of skill, because that presumes a degree of similarity between different situations. Whatever view we take of human life, we have to account for the fact that, while my reading of Homer may suffer from bizarre misunderstandings of ancient Greek civilisation, nonetheless I can interact with others who have read Homer through translations of widely differing times and places (from E. V. Rieu, Robert Graves or Robert Fagles to Chapman and Pope in English) and recognisably be discussing the same phenomenon. Texts triangulate experience and attest to some potentially universal points of reference. As Popper (1994: 33–4) remarks, 'The proponents of relativism put before us standards of mutual understanding which are unrealistically high. And when we fail to meet those standards, they claim that understanding is impossible'.

What is necessary is a reassertion of the possibility of a fruitful interplay between empirical evidence and theory-building, while recognising the con-tingency and groundedness of linguistic behaviour. To do this requires close attention to problems defined by practice without abandoning a commitment to careful, and necessarily tentative generalisation. Anything less would trivialise our task.

But exploring such a solution demands a follow-up paper.

Note

1. This is a condensed text of the first two-thirds of the Pit Corder Lecture. The final part will be developed into a separate paper.

14   LANGUAGE AND EDUCATION

Brindley, S. (ed.) (1994) *Teaching English*. London: Routledge in association with Open University.

Brumfit, C. J. (1995a) People's choice and language rights: EFL in language policy. Plenary Lecture to IATEFL Conference, University of York, April.

— (1995b) Teacher professionalism and research. In G. Cook and B. Seidlhofer (eds) *Principle and Practice in Applied Linguistics* (pp. 27–41). Oxford: Oxford University Press.

Buckingham, T. and Eskey, D. E. (1980) Towards a definition of applied linguistics. In R. B. Kaplan (ed.) *On the Scope of Applied Linguistics* (pp. 1–3). Rowley, MA: Newbury House.

Carter, R. A. (1990) Introduction. In R. A. Carter (ed) *Knowledge about Language and the Curriculum: The LINC Reader* (pp. 1–20). London: Hodder and Stoughton.

Cook, G. and Seidlhofer, B. (eds) (1995) *Principle and Practice in Applied Linguistics*. Oxford: Oxford University Press.

Corder, S. Pit (1973) *Introducing Applied Linguistics*. Harmondsworth: Penguin.

Crystal, D. (1980) *A First Dictionary of Linguistics and Phonetics*. London: Deutsch.

— (1981) *Directions in Applied Linguistics*. London: Academic Press.

— (1987) *The Cambridge Encyclopedia of Language*. Cambridge: Cambridge University Press.

Gregersen, F. (1991) Relationships between linguistics and applied linguistics: Some Danish examples. In R. Phillipson, E. Kellerman, L. Selinker, M. Sharwood Smith and M. Swain (eds) *Foreign/Second Language Pedagogy Research* (pp. 11–28). Clevedon: Multilingual Matters.

Halliday, M. A. K., McIntosh, A. and Strevens, P. D. (1964) *The Linguistic Sciences and Language Teaching*. Harlow: Longman.

Hamilton, E. and Cairns, H. (1961) *The Collected Dialogues of Plato*. Princeton: Princeton University Press.

Howatt, A. P. R. (1984) *A History of English Language Teaching*. Oxford: Oxford University Press.

Kaplan, R. B. (1980) On the scope of linguistics, applied and non-. In R. B. Kaplan (ed.) *On the Scope of Applied Linguistics* (pp. 57–66). Rowley, MA: Newbury House.

Kaplan, R. B. and Widdowson, H. G. (1992) Applied linguistics. In W. Bright (ed.) *International Encyclopedia of Linguistics*, Volume 1. New York and Oxford: Oxford University Press.

Krashen, S. D. (1980) Towards a redefinition of applied linguistics. In R. B. Kaplan (ed.) *On the Scope of Applied Linguistics* (pp. 12–13). Rowley, MA: Newbury House.

Mackey, W. F. (1966) Applied linguistics: Its meaning and use. *English Language Teaching* 20 (1), 197–206. Cited from J. P. B. Allen and S. Pit Corder (eds) (1973) *Readings for Applied Linguistics, The Edinburgh Course in Applied Linguistics*, Volume 1 (pp. 247–55). Oxford: Oxford University Press.

Mitchell, R. F., Brumfit, C. J. and Hooper, J. (1994) 'Knowledge about Language': Policy, rationales and practices. *Research Papers in Education* 9(2), 183–205.

Palmer, J. D. (1980) Linguistics in *Medias Res*. In R. B. Kaplan (ed) *On the Scope of Applied Linguistics* (pp. 21–27). Rowley, MA: Newbury House.

Pennycook, A. (1994) *The Cultural Politics of English as an International Language*. Harlow: Longman.

Phillipson, R. (1992) *Linguistic Imperialism*. Oxford: Oxford University Press.

Plato (*c* 400 BC) *Philebus*. In E. Hamilton and H. Cairns (eds) *The Collected Dialogues of Plato* (pp. 1086–150). Princeton: Princeton University Press.

Politzer, R. L. (1972) *Linguistics and Applied Linguistics: Aims and methods.* Concord, MA: Heinle and Heinle.

Popper, K. R. (1994) *The Myth of the Framework.* London: Routledge.

Richards, J. C., Platt, J. and Platt, H. (1985) *Longman Dictionary of Applied Linguistics.* Harlow: Longman (2nd edn, 1992 as *Longman Dictionary of Language Teaching and Applied Linguistics*).

Robins, R. H. (1967) *A Short History of Linguistics.* Harlow: Longman.

Spolsky, B. (1978) *Educational Linguistics.* Rowley, MA: Newbury House.

Stern, H. H. (1983) *Fundamental Concepts of Language Teaching.* Oxford: Oxford University Press.

Strevens, P. (1975) Statement for AILA. Reprinted in R. B. Kaplan (ed.) (1980) *On the Scope of Applied Linguistics* (pp. 17–20). Rowley, MA: Newbury House.

Stubbs, M. (1986) *Educational Linguistics.* Oxford: Blackwell.

Swarbrick, A. (ed.) (1994) *Teaching Modern Languages.* London: Routledge in association with Open University.

Tollefson, J. W. (1991) *Planning Language, Planning Inequality: Language policy in the community.* London: Longman.

Wardhaugh, R. (1974) *Topics in Applied Linguistics.* Rowley, MA: Newbury House.

Widdowson, H. G. (1979) *Explorations in Applied Linguistics.* Oxford: Oxford University Press.

— (1980) Models and fictions. *Applied Linguistics* 1(2), 165–70.

2 Second Language Acquisition Theory Building?

JAMES P. LANTOLF
Cornell University

Introduction

This is a paper about a punctuation mark; not in the sense of the interesting paper by Bruthiaux (1995) on the semicolon, which appeared in *Applied Linguistics,* but in the sense of why something seemingly as important as SLA theory building should be questioned in the first place. After all, theory building is good thing to do; or is it?

A number of SLA scholars have begun to focus their energies on the concern with a theory, or theories, of SLA (see Beretta, 1991; Beretta & Crookes, 1993; Crookes, 1992; Eubank & Gregg, 1995; Gregg, 1989, 1993; Long, 1985, 1993; Spolsky, 1985, 1990), presumably because the field has reached a sufficient level of maturity, empirical richness and sophistication that in order to legitimize itself as a science it needs a centripetal core around which the work of its researchers can coalesce. Others have worried not so much about the shape of SLA theory or theories as they have about the interface between theory and practice (Clarke, 1994; van Lier, 1991, 1994; Pennycook, 1990, 1994, among others). Still others, especially Schumann (1983), have wondered whether the entire enterprise of theory building is even worth the effort, given the 'relative' (and I use the term with due caution at this point) unimportance of the field.

What I want to do here is to address the literature whose concern is to imbue the field with a proper sense of theory, and consequently, of science. Hence, the primary focus of my remarks will be on the writings of Beretta, Crookes, Long, Gregg, Eubank, and Schumann.

The modern scientific enterprise, which provides the macrostructure for the SLA theory-building literature, has its roots in the Enlightenment, a philosophical

16

credo that brought to the fore reason, rationality, the universal, objectivity and the search for the truth. We find all of these elements permeating the writings of those concerned with SLA theory building. Their assumption seems to be that following these beliefs will lead to explanation, understood in causal terms, and will ultimately give rise to the truth about SLA. I am convinced that the proposals espoused by those currently seeking to build SLA theory have to be challenged, if for no other reason than they present a rather biased and uncritical view of things. Such is the project of the present paper.

Physics Envy

I am certainly not the first, nor do I pretend to be the most capable of challenging the tenets of modern science. Others have been engaged in this task for a lot longer and have done a much better job than I could ever do, and I draw heavily on their work.

SLA theory builders propose to confer an air of legitimacy upon the discipline by tying it to the apron strings of the natural sciences. Beretta & Crookes (1993: 271, n. 7), for example, in arguing for the importance of separating theory from practice, make the following statement: 'If SLA is to take its cue from the natural sciences (as Chomskyan linguists think linguistics should do), then it cannot be guided, inhibited, or distracted by practical concerns'; and also in the same note, they continue 'No one expects a theoretical physicist to attend to engineering nor theorists working on the Human Genome Project to attend to medicine'. Furthermore, Gregg, Beretta, Long, and Crookes cite work in Newtonian physics, plate tectonics, and relativity theory as evidence of how scientists construct theories.

It seems to me, however, that the theory builders are suffering from a bad case of what Gould (1981: 262) calls 'physics envy'. This is all the more interesting when one considers that researchers in other human science, including anthropology, sociology, psychology and cognitive science, have for some time realized that the natural sciences might not be the most appropriate model to follow for their theoretical inspiration (Polkinghorne, 1988). Hence, philosophers like Gergen, Leary, Lather, and Best and Kellner, among others, argue that science is a matter of the production and interpretation of texts. To appreciate what this means, I would like to consider a particular kind of scientific text – the text known as *theory*.

Metaphor as Theory

Gregg opens his (1989) paper on generativism in SLA research, with the seemingly uncontroversial comment (although see van Lier, 1991, 1994; Ellis,

1995) that 'The ultimate goal of second language acquisition research is the development of a theory of second language acquisition'. Beretta (1993: 221) echoes this view when he writes, 'Theory construction is the normal activity (whether implicit or explicit) of any scientist in formulating explanatory principles'. Although Gregg (1993: 277) believes that research can be carried out in the absence of theory, it is better if you have one to guide you because it provides a set of interesting questions, a way of determining the explanandum and a set of statements (explanans) to explain how or why things are the way they are. Theories are supposed to lead us to the truth.

In the case of SLA, according to Gregg, the explanandum is the acquisition of L2 competence and the explanans is some as yet undiscovered mechanism – a mechanism that supposedly causes acquisition (1993: 278). Gregg contends, however, that before we can worry about the mechanism through which acquisition happens, we need to explain precisely what it is that acquirers acquire. Therefore, we need a theory of linguistic competence, and for Gregg (1989, 1993) the only theory of competence worth considering is Chomsky's, because it is the most developed and scientifically sophisticated of all linguistic theories. Eubank & Gregg (1995: 51) go even further in proclaiming UG theory as '*the only one there is*' and therefore it must be taken seriously (1995: 54). This is a pretty good metaphysical move, because, as Eubank & Gregg (1995: 54) state, it allows us to 'transcend loose talk of proficiency, ability, "communicative competence".'

In his insightful response to Eubank & Gregg's (1995) criticism of his neurobiological L2 research, Schumann (1995: 61) reminds us that what has to be taken seriously is language, not linguistics and that language entails much more than knowledge of a set of permissible sentences, specifically what it is that people need to learn to be able to interact with other people from different cultures and speech communities.

With regard to the supposed plethora of current SLA theories (see Long, 1985), Gregg (1993: 289) remarks that most of them 'are not in fact really theories, but rather either descriptive, non-explanatory frameworks for L2 researchers on the one hand, or else *metaphors* [emphasis added] for organizing one's thoughts on the other'. Some ten years earlier Schumann (1983: 54) suggested considering SLA constructs as 'literary *metaphors*' rather than as fullblown 'scientific constructs'. I would like to argue that indeed both Gregg and Schumann are correct in implicitly, at least, relating scientific theories, SLA or otherwise, to metaphors, and further that metaphors, including those discursively elevated to the status of theory, are, and this is the key point, used for organizing our thoughts. This final point applies to scientists and their thoughts as much as it does to everybody else (Lakoff & Johnson, 1980: 185). As Gergen (1990: 267) puts it, 'Indeed, without metaphor, scientific thinking as a whole would remain paralyzed'.

The history of the Western scientific tradition from its roots in Plato and Aristotle shows quite clearly the central role played by metaphor (Leary, 1990; Smith, 1990). Some of the preeminent thinkers in the natural sciences relied heavily on metaphors, and in a curious twist, constructed their metaphors of the physical world from their observations of the social world. Newton's concept of universal gravitation, for example, conceptualized the movement of masses of matter toward each other 'as analogous to the "attraction" of human persons toward one another' (Leary, 1990: 10), and Darwin relied on the comparison between the breeding of animals controlled by humans and 'the putatively natural selection of variants carried out by Nature' (Leary, 1990: 11). Many scholars, including Einstein, have recognized the metaphorical quality inherent in as sacred a discipline as mathematics and have realized that the application of numbers to a problem, whether in pure or applied research, is a rhetorical tactic intended to persuade rather than to present a definite account of reality (Leary, 1990: 33, n. 19).

Despite the pervasiveness of metaphor in scientific thinking, or perhaps because of it, scholars from very early on have been trying, unsuccessfully, to purge science of this insidious deterrent to clear and objective thinking. In doing so, however, they have been themselves unable to avoid use of metaphors (Leary, 1990; Smith, 1990). Noteworthy here are the logical positivists, who relegated metaphors to the third discursive category of nonsensical expressions (the first two consisting of logical and empirical propositions, respectively), but were still unable to sustain their anti-metaphorical position, using such phrases as *logical atoms, molecular proposition, picture theory of meaning, machine for grinding out theorems, soil of observation, empirical foundation,* and *plane of empirical facts* (Smith, 1990: 240).

Crookes (1992) recognizes the central role that metaphor plays in theory building. While Crookes and I are in agreement here, we disagree on the crucial point of when metaphors enter into the theory construction process. As *I* read Crookes (1992: 432), theories are cognitive objects arising in the scientist's mind *prior* to their linguistic or logical formulations in the form of analogies and models. Crookes' perspective is based on the received view in science, which holds that the mind imposes structure on thought and language; thus, the conduit metaphor: 'put thoughts into words'. A postmodernist, or even a Vygotskian, take on cognition, however, reverses the relationship between mind and language: language and metaphorical concepts (Lakoff & Johnson, 1980: 3; Harre & Gillette, 1994: 123) impose structure on the mind; thus, a new metaphor: 'put words into thoughts' (see Vygotsky, 1986). In this view, were it not for culturally constructed metaphorical concepts, theorizing would be impossible.

The Myth of Literalization

Theories are metaphors that have achieved the status of acceptance by a group of people we refer to as scientists. The process through which metaphors are accepted by scientists is known as literalization, or mythification – a process which entails the crucial step of erasing the *as if* (Leary, 1990: 47, n. 49). Literalization is in turn based on the belief that 'proper theories are literal, logical constructs, which is itself an abstract metaphor' (Hoffman *et al.*, 1990: 212).

It is generally assumed that metaphorical language derives its meaning from its opposition to literal language, where literal language is seen to directly represent the phenomena to which it refers (Gergen, 1990: 268). Stated in this way, we can appreciate why scientists have struggled so mightily, if in vain, to develop a literal discourse (1990: 268). Literalists have then consistently worried about a hearer or reader understanding a speaker's or writer's utterance or sentence 'as meaning something other than its literal objective meaning' (Lakoff & Johnson, 1980: 206). Yet, 'the distinction between literal and metaphoric language is specious', given that metaphorical language depends for its very existence on literal language – without literal language there can be no metaphor (Gergen, 1990: 269).

Basing his argumentation on Wittgenstein's notion of language 'games' (the details of which I leave aside), Gergen proposes that literal language is 'essentially any constituent of an established or reiterative pattern (word–action–object)', or 'in other words, literal words are simply those that occupy an established position in a language game that is repeated with some kind of regularity' to the point where they eventually 'feel right' or where 'they seem to "reflect" the world' (1990: 270). To ponder the meaning of a word is not to worry about its referents nor the speaker's or writer's intentions but to contemplate the 'fuller set of practices in which the term is embedded on a particular occasion', and metaphor arises when the regularized, 'culturally sedimented' pattern is altered (1990: 270). Although 'a new term thrust into an alien context will seem metaphoric at the outset', as it is eventually integrated into the common practice of a community, it takes on a literal character (1990: 270). Quite often searching out the term's origins will bring to light its metaphorical dimension (1990: 270). Seemingly literal scientific terms like 'gravity', 'linguistic competence', and 'correlation', have become literal within the respective scientific communities that use them, not because they capture reality, but because they allow scientists to 'coordinate their activities across time and circumstance' (Gergen, 1990: 271).

The greater the acceptance of and acquiescence to standard scientific language within a discipline, the greater the chances that the productivity of the scientific endeavor will diminish. Hence, to keep a field fresh and vibrant, one must create new metaphors, which maintain some conventions while simultaneously violating others (Gergen, 1990: 272). Thus, the 40 to 60 metaphors and models populating SLA may not be all that bad to the extent that they maintain the field's vitality.

In cautioning against the use of metaphors in SLA, Gregg (1993: 291, n. 16) cites a statement by Fodor and Pylyshyn in which these authors assert that reliance on metaphor often confers 'license to take one's claims as something less than serious hypotheses'. In the light of the foregoing discussion, however, it seems clear that without metaphor, there would be no scientific theory. In a sense, to develop a theory one must behave precisely in a contrary manner to what Fodor and Pylyshyn contend; that is, one must take one's metaphor seriously and succeed in convincing others to take it seriously as well, in order to elevate it to the status of scientific theory. A decisive step in achieving this is the erasure of the *as if* from the metaphor, thus rendering the metaphor literal. But, as I have already mentioned, the danger in taking this step is the mythification of the metaphor (see Barthes, 1962).

So, it seems we have the answer to the ? of my title: SLA theory building, like all scientific theory building, is about taking metaphors seriously; in other words, it is about incorporating metaphors into scientific practice through repetition and subsequently mythologizing them into literal language.

Truth and 'Relativaphobia'

Despite the claim that science has cast off the coils of positivism, it seems clear that many of its beliefs continue to exert their influence on SLA. Falsificationism, although questioned by some (see Long, 1993; Beretta, 1991) and even rejected by others in favor of exploration (see Schumann, 1993), still guides, if only implicitly, much experimental research. Moreover, the absolutist belief in a single reality existing 'out there' as well as belief in the objectivity of scientific practice and progress toward the ultimate truth are alive and well.[1] Long (1993: 233–4), for instance, writes that 'the increasing accuracy of predictions suggests when the theorist is getting closer to the truth'. He also states that even though research results are normally reported in 'theory-dependent language, the physical results of experiments themselves depend on the way the world is, not the theory that motivated them, nor the strength of the researcher's belief in the theory' (1993: 233). Gregg (1993: 291, n. 10) takes an even stronger stance in his rejection of the theory-ladenness of observation as a 'red herring', supporting his contention with a recent experimental study carried out by Eubank designed to test sentence processing constraints via grammaticality judgments of sentences flashed on a computer screen (Gregg, 1993: 284). For Gregg not only is Eubank's study free from theoretical colouring; it is also observation free, since it uses a computer to record responses and carry out statistical analysis. If this doesn't beg the question, I don't know what does. I am quite sure the computer did not set up the study, nor did it force Eubank to carry out a statistical comparison of judgments on sentences. None other than Popper (1981) dismisses pure, theory-free, observation as a ludicrous supposition and argues that what scientists observe is a function of what they are searching for.

Beretta (1991: 502), although strongly desiring the contrary, at least acknow-ledges that observation is theory laden and that 'relativism may be inevitable'. Ellis (1995: 88) echoes a similar view in commenting that theories are not con-textless creations but are developed by specific groups of researchers with specific intentions and purposes (e.g. the desire of some to establish firm ties with mainstream linguistics). Beretta argues that there may be 'a better basis for belief in one theory than another' and that one theory may be more successful at solving problems than another (1991: 502). But theories can often suggest the existence of the very problems they are supposedly designed to solve (see Yngve, 1986 on linguistic theory).

Beretta's worries about theory-ladenness and of what I call *relativaphobia*, or the irrational fear 'that there is no uniquely privileged position from which to know' (Usher & Edwards, 1994: 37) are pervasive in the SLA theory building literature.[2] Its roots reside in the assumption that difference and heterogeneity are impediments to mastery of the truth (Usher & Edwards, 1994: 37). Only Schumann (1983), as far as I can tell, dared to advocate an openly relativistic stance on SLA theory in the name of an aesthetics rather than a science of SLA.[3] Throughout his paper, he clearly argues for a (modified or perhaps cautious) constructivist position on model building. At one point he writes 'now the question is whether this formulation [Perdue's depiction of the development of pragmatic into syntactic speech] describes a reality or whether it creates one' and 'although Figure 1 does not represent pure creation, for several reasons, I think we can argue that there is substantial creation involved' (1983: 64). Near the end of his paper, however, he seems to slide away from a strong relativist posture stating that 'all these drawings [i.e. models for SLA] are attempts to depict the same reality (SLA)' (1983: 67), and then concludes that since we cannot determine whether symbolic realism or positivism is ultimately correct, we ought to adopt both positions and engage in SLA research as an art and as a science (1983: 68). In Beretta's opinion (1991: 495), Schumann's position is an extreme form of nihilism and is to be shunned.[4]

Much of what has been written by SLA theory builders is directed at ridding the field of its relativistic personality. Hence, authors such as Long, Crookes and Beretta suggest ways of culling the field of its superabundance of theories, models and metaphors. According to Long (1993: 228), incommensurable theories (those based on radically different underlying SLA realities, presumably the case for variable competence models versus homogeneous competence models), must be eliminated, while complementary theories (acculturation models and UG models, perhaps ?), which supposedly account for different aspects of the same reality, should be saved. Beretta (1991: 497), who expresses a parallel viewpoint, contends that in the successful (presumably, hard) sciences, 'single theories tend to dominate'. The implication for the field of SLA is transparent.

Long (1993), recognizing the inherent dangers of a single-theory science (suggesting that it could give rise to a Hitlerian *Neue Welt Ordnung*), tempers this stance in observing that in the history of any scientific field, there generally coexists a triad of theories – a dominant theory, a competing theory, and an alternative to both (p. 229). Apparently, relativism is not so bad after all, provided it is a constrained relativism. In my view, however, it is not the maximum or minimum number of theories that matters, but the attitude of the scientists espousing them. The danger resides not in the number of theories, complementary or otherwise, but in the scientists' adoption of an absolutist posture which posits a single reality and assumes that theirs is the true theory corresponding to that reality.

In his assault on absolutism, Adorno (1983) traces its origins to the need of bourgeois philosophers to compensate 'for their own lack of material grounding' and legitimize their existence by proclaiming 'an absolute ground for knowledge'; thus bequeathing to themselves intellectual *property* (Best & Kellner, 1991: 231). Above all, according to Adorno, it is the 'quest for certainty and foundations' that can give rise to the tyranny of 'authoritarian personalities' and ultimately lead to the kind of *Neue Welt Ordnung* that Long so justifiably fears. As Brown (1994: 27) points out, the world has witnessed far fewer atrocities as a result of excessive tolerance than it has as a consequence of abolutism.

Given the relationship between metaphor and theory as I have outlined it above, the relativistic view of things is not only plausible but represents a serious challenge to, if not the complete undermining of, the hegemony enjoyed by the absolutism and foundationalism of modern scientific theorizing and practice (see Gergen, 1994: 58). Thus the relativism that Long, Beretta, Crookes and Gregg so eagerly seek to avoid may already be upon us.

A strong relativist view holds that theories as regularized, often mythologized, metaphors, create through linguistic means the very reality they seek to explain. Some late modernist scholars, such as Adorno and Lakoff & Johnson (1980), adopt a more moderate view, which supports a single, but only partially knowable, reality – partially knowable because our observations are always and everywhere mediated by society, objects, and above all, by language.

While the mediational perspective might be a safe middle ground to occupy, I nevertheless find merit in the contention of the antirepresentational constructivist stance that emphasizes multiple realities and denounces claims to theoretical superiority and absolute truth espoused by the grand narratives of modern science (see Rosenau, 1992: 80). But in allowing for multiple, and often incommensurable, theories, isn't the spectre of relativism, or indeed, nihilism, now given free reign? I think it is possible to allay people's fears, while at the same time maintaining the relativist posture I have been arguing for in SLA.

First of all, we have to recognize, as Lather (1992) observes, that relativism and nihilism are concepts emanating from the modern foundationalist discourse that 'posits grounds for certainty outside of context, some neutral, disinterested, stable point of reference' (1992: 99) and masks the role of power and arrogance in producing truth, rather than discovering truth covered, which in turn imbues the power holders with even more power. In Western science, the producers of truth, not too surprisingly, have by and large been white class-privileged males (Lather, 1992: 100).

Second, we need to distinguish epistemic from judgmental relativism. The former recognizes that knowledge is always and everywhere constructed and moulded by specific historical and social circumstances and that this knowledge cannot be extra-linguistically described. The latter clearly differentiates itself from the former in its insistence that because all knowledge is situated, and thus shaped by socio-historical and linguistic forces, it is all equally valid, and thus it is illegitimate to compare and discriminate among different kinds of knowledge (Brown, 1994: 27). The epistemic view refuses to accept the judgmental stance and contends that we can distinguish among different forms of knowledge in terms of their relevance and adequacy for attaining particular goals. Some forms of knowledge are more successful at solving practical problems and others at explaining specific phenomena (1994: 27). How do we decide which forms of knowledge are indeed more successful in realizing the intended goal? This is achieved not through logical, computational argumentation but through rational social discourse. The fact that truth is then socially constructed and thus situated does not make it untrue (Brown, 1994: 22). It does, however, mean that ways of determining truth are constructed, at times cooperatively and at times conflictively, through discursive practices which, because they are socio-historical in nature, are constantly reviewed and periodically reshaped (1994: 22). All of this means that truth is not discovered but invented.

If theories are not getting us closer to the truth what good are they? A postmodernist answer might be that while theories do not deserve the reverence they enjoy in modern science, they do matter because they are invitations for scientists to engage in discussions (Rosenau, 1992: 82), aimed at working out discursive forms that serve their local needs (Gergen, 1990: 294). Hence, the goal of science is not about the uncovering of a single truth about a single reality but 'different forms of intelligibility or understanding, each with restricted, practical value' (Gergen, 1990: 294). Interest now shifts from truth existing independently of its explanation to how the explanation is constructed and made adequate. The search for the Holy Grail, therefore, is still on; only the telos is not the grail but the quest itself. As Brown (1994: 33) puts it, 'the ideal republic did exist for Plato and his friends in their quest, in their actual practice of talking about it'.

Conclusion: Let All the Flowers Bloom

It seems appropriate to conclude this discussion with a metaphor. The picture of the future of SLA as painted in the papers on theory building is, in my opinion, rather stark. I think Long (1993: 230) captures this view quite nicely, in what I hope remains as a utopian image of our field as one populated by researchers satisfied with their theory, 'at peace with themselves and each other over basic issues in the philosophy of science', and therefore having nothing left to do but attend to the details and harvest the applications of the theory; that is, they engage in the business of normal science. SLA came into its own contemporaneously with the rise of postmodernism. Is it merely a coincidence that the field is so incredibly, and happily from my perspective, diverse, creative, often contentious, and always full of controversy?

Insistence on a definitive theory or even a small number of commensurable theories is a potentially abusive position to the extent that it cuts off alternative metaphors (Leary, 1990: 40, n. 35) and often leads to domination by, and mythification of, a single, official, metaphor. According to Leary (1990: 40), 'the metaphors bandied about today with such confidence by psychologists and cognitive scientists may infiltrate public consciousness (and personal self-consciousness) and remain lodged there, long after these same psychologists and cognitive scientists have adopted a new set of metaphors'. It seems clear, then, that we must let all the flowers bloom, not just a select few. You never know which ones will attract the eye of researchers to become tomorrow's realities (Gergen, 1990: 295).

Notes

1. For the time being, I leave aside the problem of 'progress', also part of the positivist legacy in science; nevertheless, because of it illusory properties, it is an issue that must be eventually addressed (see Rosenau, 1992).
2. Perhaps a gentler way of putting things would be to say that it is not so much that relativism is feared as it is that it leads to feelings of nostalgia for lost foundations and fixed rules of conduct (Brown, 1994: 23); however, SLA is still probably too young to

experience strong feelings of nostalgia for something lost and thus I think fear is a
more appropriate way of capturing the anti-relativistic position of many in our field.
3. Van Lier (1994) and Spolsky (1990) argue for theoretical pluralism in SLA and thus
avoid the negative baggage affiliated with relativism.
4. Happily for those suffering from relativaphobia, according to Long (1993: 242, n. 5),
Schumann recanted his relativist ways at a 1992 conference and openly declared
himself to be a realist.

References

Adorno, T. W. (1983) *Against Epistemology*. London: Blackwell.

Barthes, R. (1962) *Mythologies*. New York: Hill and Wang.

Beretta, A. (1991) Theory construction in SLA: Complementarity and opposition. *Studies in Second Language Acquisition* 13, 493–511.

— (1993) 'As God said, and I think, rightly ...' Perspectives on theory consruction in SLA: An introduction. *Applied Linguistics* 11, 221–4.

Beretta, A. and Crookes, G. (1993) Cognitive and social determinants of discovery in SLA. *Applied Linguistics* 14, 250–75.

Best, S. and Kellner, D. (1991) *Postmodern Theory. Critical interrogations.* New York: Guilford.

Brown, R. H. (1994) Reconstructing social theory after the postmodern critique. In H. W. Simons and M. Billig (eds) *After Postmodernism. Reconstructing ideology critique* (pp. 12–37). London: Sage.

Bruthiaux, P. (1995) The rise and fall of the semicolon: English punctuation theory and English teaching practice. *Applied Linguistics* 16, 1–14.

Clarke, M. A. (1994) The dysfunctions of the theory/practice discourse. *TESOL Quarterly* 28, 9–26.

Crookes, G. (1992) Theory format and SLA theory. *Studies in Second Language Acquisition* 14, 425–49.

Ellis, R. (1995) Appraising second language acquisition theory in relation to language pedagogy. In G. Cook and B. Seidlhofer (eds) *Principle and Practice in Applied Linguistics. Studies in honour of H. G. Widdowson* (pp. 73–90). Oxford: Oxford University Press.

Eubank, L. and Gregg, K. R. (1995) 'Et in amygdala ego'? UG, (S)LA, and neurobiology. *Studies in Second Language Acquisition* 17, 35–57.

Gergen, K. J. (1990) Metaphor, metatheory, and the social world. In D. E. Leary (ed.) *Metaphors in the History of Psychology* (pp. 267–99). Cambridge: Cambridge University Press.

— (1994) The limits of pure critique. In H. W. Simons and M. Billig (eds) *After Postmodernism. Reconstructing ideology critique* (pp. 58–78). London: Sage.

Gould, S. J. (1981) *The Mismeasure of Man*. New York: Norton.

Gregg, K. (1989) Second language acquisition theory: The case for a generative perspective. In S. M. Gass and J. Schachter (eds) *Linguistic Perspectives on Second Language Acquisition* (pp. 15–40). Cambridge: Cambridge University Press.

— (1993) Taking explanation seriously; or, let a couple of flowers bloom. *Applied Linguistics* 14, 276–94.

Harre, R. and Gillette, G. (1994) *The Discursive Mind*. Thousand Oaks, CA: Sage.

Hoffman, R. R., Cochran, E. L. and Nead, J. M. (1990) Cognitive metaphors in experimental psychology. In D. E. Leary (ed.) *Metaphors in the History of Psychology* (pp. 173–229). Cambridge: Cambridge University Press.

Lakoff, G. and Johnson, M. (1980) *Metaphors We Live By.* Chicago: University of Chicago Press.

Lather, P. (1992) Postmodernism and the human sciences. In S. Kvale (ed.) *Postmodern Psychology* (pp. 88–109). London: Sage.

Leary, D. E. (1990) Psyche's muse: The role of metaphor in the history of psychology. In D. E. Leary (ed.) *Metaphors in the History of Psychology* (pp. 1–78). Cambridge: Cambridge University Press.

Long, M. H. (1985) Input and second language acquisition theory. In S. Gass and C. Madden (eds) *Input in Second Language Acquisition Theory* (pp. 377–93). Rowley, MA: Newbury House.

— (1993) Assessment strategies for second language acquisition theories. *Applied Linguistics* 14, 225–49.

Pennycook, A. (1990) Towards a critical applied linguistics for the 1990s. *Issues in Applied Linguistics* 1, 8–28.

— (1994) Incommensurable discourses? *Applied Linguistics* 15, 115–38.

Polkinghorne, D. E. (1988) *Narrative Knowing and the Human Sciences.* Albany, NY: State University of New York Press.

Popper, K. (1981) The myth of inductive hypothesis generation. In R. D. Tweney, M. E. Doherty and C. R. Mynatt (eds) *On Scientific Thinking* (pp. 72–6). New York: Columbia University Press.

Rosenau, P. M. (1992) *Post-Modernism and the Social Sciences. Insights, inroads and intrusions.* Princeton, NJ: Princeton University Press.

Schumann, J. H. (1983) Art and science in second language acquisition research. *Language Learning* 33, 49–76.

— (1993) Some problems with falsification: An illustration from SLA research. *Applied Linguistics* 14, 295–306.

— (1995) Ad minorem theoriae gloriam. A response to Eubank and Gregg. *Studies in Second Language Acquisition* 17, 59–63.

Smith, L. D. (1990) Metaphors of knowledge and behavior in the behaviorist tradition. In D. E. Leary (ed.) *Metaphors in the History of Psychology* (pp. 239–66). Cambridge: Cambridge University Press.

Spolsky, B. (1985) Formulating a theory of second language learning. *Studies in Second Language Acquisition* 7, 269–88.

— (1990) Introduction to a colloquium: The scope and form of a theory of second language learning. *TESOL Quarterly* 24, 609–16.

Usher, R. and Edwards, R. (1994) *Postmodernism and Education.* London: Routledge.

van Lier, L. (1991) Doing applied linguistics: Towards a theory of practice. *Issues in Applied Linguistics* 2, 78–81.

— (1994) Forks and hope: Pursuing understanding in different ways. *Applied Linguistics* 15, 328–46.

Vygotsky, L. S. (1986) *Thought and Language.* Cambridge, MA: MIT Press.

Yngve, V. H. (1986) *Linguistics as a Science.* Bloomington, IN: Indiana University Press.

3 Language and the Guided Construction of Knowledge

NEIL MERCER
The Open University

Introduction

This paper is about language and the guided construction of knowledge. By this I mean that I am concerned with the role of language in the social process of teaching and learning, and more specifically with spoken language in schools. What I have to say is related to three main topics:

(1) Language and thinking;

(2) How teachers use talk to teach;

(3) How children use talk to learn.

I will deal with these topics in turn, to some extent; but I think that in the applied study of language in education they should not be kept separate. I believe that further progress in developing our understanding of the role of language in classroom education will come from a consideration of the whole communicative process of 'teaching-and-learning'. Here are three propositions, which I will go on to elaborate:

(1) Human learning is commonly a social, rather than an individual, activity;

(2) Intellectual development is essentially a culturally-situated, guided process;

(3) Becoming educated is largely a matter of learning certain 'ways with words'.

Language and Thinking

Before looking at events in schools, I want to make some more general observations about language and thinking. It is quite common for people to contrast

28

'talking' with 'doing' – 'he's all talk, he never gets things done'. But 'talking' can be 'doing', of course, a form of social action. People use spoken language to account for themselves, to pursue their interests and try and make other people do what they want. Such ideas have been explored in an interesting line of pragmatics research, from philosophers (e.g. Austin, 1962) through the ethnomethodologists (e.g. Schegloff *et al.,* 1977) into the currently influential work of conversation analysts (e.g. Drew & Heritage, 1992). But talk is not just a form of social action, it is also *a social mode of thinking* – a means by which humans can jointly construct knowledge and understanding (Mercer, 1995). Human beings use talk to give ideas a form of reality, to dispute them, to share them and develop them together; they use language to construct cultures. People collectively create and establish language practices for doing so. It is this capability for organizing ways of thinking together, as much as any other, which is the distinguishing characteristic of the intelligence of our species.

Of course, thinking is also something that is self-evidently individual: we all can and do do it in the privacy of our own heads. But any model of human thinking which does not recognize it also as a social, and as a socialized, activity, must be woefully inadequate. Here is an anecdotal form of comment on how the two modes of thinking, individual and social, are intertwined. One time, close to my daughter's third birthday, I was sitting reading the paper while she played. The following conversation then took place:

Anna: Daddy, will you play with me?

(no reply)

Anna: Daddy will you play with me?

(no reply)

Anna: Daddy! Daddy will you play? *(pause)* She said to her daddy.

With her last remark, she succeeded in getting my attention, which was one of the things she was using language to try to do. But what else was she doing here? The effect of her final statement was to put the rest of what she had said into inverted commas. I think that she was drawing on her early experience of written language – the storybooks that were read to her – to recast and reinterpret her current experience. To use a neo-Vygotskian concept, Anna *appropriated* the language of a storybook, and used it both to think with and to communicate with me (Leont'ev, 1981; Newman *et al.,* 1989). A dynamic concept of *context* (Edwards & Mercer, 1987) is also relevant and useful here – context as information which speakers share to support the meanings of their talk. The *contemporaneous context* for Anna's talk was provided by our location, and what we were both doing at the time. But a *historical context* for the talk was provided by the storytelling we did together. And that past experience of storytelling had also provided her with some cultural, linguistic resources for dealing with the present situation. An important purpose of education is to help students gain and use such cultural, linguistic resources so that they can use language effectively, as both a social and an individual mode of thinking.

Language and Education

The study of language and the guided construction of knowledge can usefully draw on several lines of research, spread across several disciplines. I will review these briefly here. The first line of research is psychological. I write at a time when someone who died more than 60 years ago is being very influential in psychological and educational research: the Russian Lev Vygotsky. Vygotsky argued persuasively that human psychological development is essentially a communicative, culturally-situated process (Vygotsky, 1978). Neo-Vygotskians like Jerome Bruner (e.g. 1985) and David Wood (1988) have more recently developed the notion of adults' support for children's learning as 'scaffolding', the provision of a 'vicarious consciousness' which helps children reach cognitive heights they would not be able to scale alone. Barbara Rogoff (1990) and others have offered the related idea of intellectual development as a process of 'cognitive apprenticeship', and in so doing have emphasised the crucial role that language and interpersonal communication play in that process. From the point of view of language researchers, however, developmental psychologists like Bruner and Rogoff give relatively little attention to the actual linguistic communication which enables human development and learning. Moreover, most of their research has been done in homes and nurseries, and so it has only analogous relevance to research on communication in classrooms. So while the neo-Vygotskian psychologists provide some useful theoretical resources for the study of language in education, they leave language researchers with a lot of work still to do.

This brings me to a second very relevant strand of research, that of anthropologists and others who have studied language practices (e.g. Heath, 1983; Street, 1984; Bloch, 1993; Barton, 1994). Although most of that research has been concerned with written, rather than spoken, language, it demonstrates how different cultural settings, such as home and school, with their different social relations, conventions and purposes, generate quite distinctive – and sometimes conflicting – ways of using spoken and written language to represent and construct ideas. Such research emphasises the importance of examining the language of classrooms in its cultural context. Schools are places with their own cultural conventions and their own institutional imperatives. Teachers have to teach a curriculum, and are accountable for doing so: and their prime tool for this task is language. Research on language practices also supports the view that for students, 'becoming educated' is very much a matter of linguistic sociali-zation, of learning how – and when – to use language in special, contextually-specific ways.

There is also a line of curriculum-related educational research, of which Barnes's work (eg Barnes & Todd, 1977, 1995; Sheeran & Barnes, 1991) is an obvious and important example, which has looked at the special nature and function of language practices in school. And finally there is the distinctive strand of linguistic research in the Hallidayan tradition, on the analysis of genres and how they are defined, taught and learned (eg Christie, 1984; Bhatia, 1993; Swales, 1990). This too can be used to support the view that education can be considered a process of guided linguistic socialization.

I believe that these various lines of research provide resources for building an applied, interdisciplinary, socio-cultural approach to the study of language in education. Such an approach would be effective for addressing questions like:

(a) How is language used as a social mode of thinking in classrooms?

(b) What language practices are students expected to learn, and why?

(c) How can teachers effectively 'scaffold' their students' understanding of, and entry into, educated discourse?

Teachers' Talk

I want next to look at teachers' talk, and I will use a real-life example (Transcript 1, below) to do so. It is part of a lesson that colleagues and I video-recorded in a secondary school in Derbyshire (Open University, 1991a). As part of their English studies, a class of fourteen year olds were engaged in an extended computer-based communication with children in a nearby primary school. They had set up a *Star Trek* style scenario, in which the secondary students were (in groups of three) pretending to be characters stranded in time and space. They used e-mail to tell the primary children about their predicaments and to ask for help, and the young children's responses were considered and used by each group of older students to develop the story further. In Transcript 1 the English teacher is questioning one group of girls about the most recent interaction and their future plans. (Note: I have avoided the use of complex transcription con-ventions, and have punctuated the text to make it easier to read.)

Transcript 1 : Dimensions

Teacher: What about the word 'dimension', because you were going to include that in your message, weren't you?

Anne: Yeh. And there's going to be – if they go in the right room, then they'll find a letter in the floor and that'll spell 'dimension'.

Teacher: What happens if they do go in the wrong room?

Emma: Well, there's no letter in the bottom, in the floor.

Teacher: Oh God! So they've got to get it right, or that's it! (*everyone laughs*) The adventurers are stuck there for ever. And Cath can't get back to her own time. What do you mean the letters are in the room, I don't quite follow that?

Emma: On the floor, like a tile or something.

Teacher: Oh I see. Why did you choose the word 'dimension'?

Anne: Don't know. (*the 3 pupils speak together, looking to each other, seeming uncertain*)

Emma: It just came up. Just said, you know, 'dimension' and everyone agreed.

Sharon: Don't know.

Teacher: Right, because it seemed to fit in with, what, the fantasy flow, flavour?

Sharon: Yeh.

Teacher: OK. Why do they go through the maze rather than go back? I mean what motivation do they have for going through it in the first place?

Emma: Um, I think that it was the king told them that Joe would be in the maze or at the end of the maze, and they didn't go back because of Joe, think it was. I'm not sure about that.

Teacher: You've really got to sort that out. It's got to be very, very clear.

In the transcribed sequence, the teacher uses questions to draw out from the students the content of their recent e-mail message, and also some justifications for what they included in it. In some ways, her language is classic 'teacher talk'. Most of her questions are ones to which she does *not* already know the answer; but she certainly evaluates the answers she receives. We have the reliable appearance of Sinclair & Coulthard's (1975) **Initiation-Response-Feedback** (IRF) exchanges (such as the last exchange in the sequence). At one level, the teacher is simply monitoring students' activity and assessing the adequacy of their attempt to continue the communication with the younger children. But her questions are not just assessment, they are *part of her teaching*. Like many effective teachers, she is using her enquiries not only to monitor children's activity, but also to guide it. Through questions like 'Why did you choose the word "dimension"?' and 'Why do they go through the maze rather than go back?' she directs their attention to matters requiring more thought and clarification. In fact, it is only when the questions she asks are considered in context, as one element of her whole interaction with the pupils, that we can see how she uses language to guide her students' endeavours. The IRF exchanges in the sequence are not discrete *loops,* but linked up together by the meaning of their content into longer *spirals.* Through talk such as this, the teacher also creates continuities in experience, both within and between lessons.

There has been a tendency to criticise teachers for their over-reliance on the use of IRF exchanges, and of questions in general. Research shows that teachers ask a lot more questions than, say, parents interacting with young children; and Dillon (1988), Wood (1992) and others report that children's participation in talk with teachers is increased by teachers asking *fewer* questions. But one can argue that these criticisms are flawed, because people in the role of 'teacher' are not necessarily trying to do the same things with language as those being 'parents'; and the amount of lively talk in a classroom is not self-evidently a measure of the educational quality of the activities taking place. If we are to make an applied analysis of how teachers use language, we need to look at function and content as well as form. Analyses which rest only on functional categories like 'questions', on the quantification of pupils' or teachers' talk, or on the identification of certain patterns of exchange, are not good enough. There are ways of using questions and IRF exchanges which are more appropriate and useful than others, and any judgement about this can only be made by taking account of the content and context of the talk. Any analysis which equates linguistic form with communicative function must be inadequate.

The value of any teacher–pupil exchange is also a matter of pragmatics. What does it achieve? What appears to happen as a result? It is worth noting that hardly any research on language in the classroom deals adequately with the fact that all human learning, and all talk, has a history and a future. To return to Transcript 1: three consecutive, related sessions were recorded with that teacher and class. When I look through the series of transcripts, I can see certain ideas, and particular terms, recurring in the talk. They are like dolphins, coming up now and again to the surface, and in doing so revealing the underlying continuity of the talk. The talk in all classrooms is bound to be like this, to some extent. As my colleague Janet Maybin (1994) puts it, talk in any one lesson is part of one long conversation of teaching-and-learning which can run through months and perhaps even years.

The guided construction of knowledge depends on language as a means for making sense of experience and for creating continuities in experience. It is through revealing connections and continuities that teachers can transform the mere experience of children into their education. In some research I am currently doing in Mexican schools with Sylvia Rojas-Drummond and her colleagues, we have found a strong association between the extent to which teachers observably use 'spiral' IRFs and other language strategies to create and enhance continuity in teaching and learning, and the eventual problem-solving ability of the children they teach (Rojas-Drummond *et al.*, 1995).

Talk amongst Learners

I now want to consider talk between pupils or students. It is now a fairly common practice, and not only in Britain, for teachers to put students to work together for some of their time in pairs or groups. However, there has been some concern about the educational value of much group work, with some observational research suggesting that such concern may well be justified (Galton *et al.*, 1982; Galton & Williamson, 1992). As applied language researchers we might therefore ask: what kinds of language use would one hope to find when students work together?

Transcript 2 provides an example of some collaborative learning taking place. It comes from a recording I obtained through my involvement in the National Oracy Project (Open University, 1991b), and was recorded by a teacher in a south London school, who left a tape recorder running while a group of girls (aged 11 and 12) worked alone together on a maths problem. The problem is as follows:

> *You have a square sheet of card measuring 15 cm by 15 cm and you want to use it to make an open cuboid container by cutting out the corners. What is the maximum capacity the container can have?*

I want to focus on one of the four girls, the one called Emily in the transcript (A, B and C represent the others).

Transcript 2: Maximum Box

Emily: This box is bigger than what it should be 'cos if you get 15 by 15 you get 225, but if you times um 9 by 9 times 3 you still get 243 and I haven't got that much space in my box.

A: You have.

Emily: But the 15 by...

B: It can be, it can work, I think.

Emily: But surely...

B: You cut off corners.

Emily: Yeh but that surely should make it *smaller.*

B: I think that is right.

Emily: (*counting squares marked on the paper*): Hang on, 1, 2, 3, 4, 5...

C: You're not going to get 243.

Emily: I shouldn't get 243 'cos if the piece of paper only had 225 then, um...

C: Hang on, look...9 times 9 times how many was it up?

A: But don't you remember Emily it's got all this space in the middle.

Emily: Yeh, but...

A: It's got all that space in the middle.

C: It is right, Emily, it is, it should be that number.

Emily: But if I have a piece of paper with 225 squares, why should I get more?

A: Because you have all that space in the middle.

Emily: (*sounding exasperated*) No, it hasn't got anything to do with it. If my piece of paper had only 225 squares on it, I can't get more out of the same piece of paper.

A: You can because you're forgetting, things go *up* as well, not just the flat piece of paper like that.

Emily: Oh yeh.

A: It's going up.

A: It's going up

C: It's because, look, down here you've got 3 and it's going up.

A: You're going 3 up, it's getting more on it. Do you see it will be 243?

Emily: Yeh.

C: It is right, it should be.

Emily was considered to be quite good at maths by her teacher. At the point the transcript begins, the girls have made a box to the dimensions required, but Emily is unhappy that the box seems to have got 'bigger' despite having lost its corners. This is because she has a fundamental misunderstanding about what they are doing. The talk reveals that Emily does not seem to have grasped the distinction between *area* and *volume*. Or, to be more precise, she does not seem to understand how a mathematical measure of volume (which she is perfectly capable of calculating) relates to the actual capacity of a three-dimensional object. One wonders how this kind of misunderstanding could arise for a child who is apparently good at maths. One possible cause is that doing maths in class is so often a book-bound activity in which few strong connections are made with the world of concrete objects in all their shapes and sizes. The 'maximum box' activity helps overcome this by creating conditions under which Emily is required to relate her maths to material reality. But by being collaborative, it also offers her the opportunity to participate in discourse which is grounded in the practical task. It is both the talk *and* the joint activity which force her to revise and extend the contextual framework for her mathematical thinking.

Unfortunately, any evidence available suggests that open, rational, productive, curriculum-related discussion of the kind we can see in Transcript 2 is quite a rare occurrence in schools. There is also no reason to believe that most teachers do a great deal to encourage its development. Yet one of the things we must want schools to give young people is the capability and confidence to use language to think together: to construct and criticise rational arguments, to be able to work with other people to examine and evaluate what they read and hear, to find common solutions to problems. At a more specific level, an important aim of education is to enable students to participate in the ways that language is used in particular fields of knowledge. As Jay Lemke (1990) has put it, science teaching should enable students to become fluent speakers of science. They need to be given access to various academic *communities of discourse*. I am not really talking here about children learning technical vocabulary, though that can be important. There is a more profound quality to any educated discourse, to do with the style and quality of argument – the ways that evidence is presented, the ways that explanations are given, and how they are evaluated. This is not self-evident to most students, but teachers commonly act as if it is. Students cannot be expected to discover educated discourse for themselves. They need guidance, a 'scaffolding' support for their entry into educated discourses. Teachers also need to raise students' awareness about the discourses or genres they are encountering (Sheeran & Barnes, 1991; Westgate & Corden, 1993), and there are means available for doing so (see for example Brooks *et al.,* 1986; Dawes, 1995). But students also need opportunities to become confident in speaking the discourse, and this means taking part in activities without the authoritative presence of the teacher. A balance of guided and independent activity must be achieved.

In some recent research, I have been looking at the quality of children's talk when they work together in class, and at how teachers can most usefully organize and support that kind of activity. One important source of my data was a joint Open University/University of East Anglia research project *Spoken Language and New Technology* (SLANT). in which we videotaped children working together at the computer in 12 primary schools in four counties of south east

England (Fisher, 1993; Mercer, 1994). We found that computer-based activities are excellent at generating talk amongst children, but the quality of the talk was variable. Our analysis led us to typify three kinds of talk, outlined below.

Three Ways of Talking and Thinking

(1) The first way of talking is **Disputational talk**, which is characterised by disagreement and individualised decision making. There are few attempts to pool resources, or to offer constructive criticism of suggestions. Disputational talk also has some characteristic discourse features, notably short exchanges consisting of assertions and counter-assertions.

(2) Next there is **Cumulative talk**, in which speakers build positively but uncritically on what the other has said. Partners use talk to construct a 'common knowledge' by accumulation. Cumulative discourse is characterised by repetitions, confirmations and elaborations.

(3) **Exploratory talk**, in which partners engage critically but constructively with each other's ideas. Statements and suggestions are offered for joint consideration. These may be challenged and counter-challenged, but challenges are justified and alternative hypotheses are offered. Compared with the other two types, in exploratory talk *knowledge is made more publicly accountable* and *reasoning is more visible in the talk*. Progress then emerges from the eventual joint agreement reached.

'Disputational', 'cumulative' and 'exploratory' are not meant to be descriptive categories into which all observed speech can be neatly and separately coded. They are analytic categories, typifications of ways that children in the SLANT project talked together. They represent models of three *distinctive social modes of thinking*, preliminary models for understanding how actual talk (which resists neat categorization) is used by people to 'think together'. The kind of talk we saw in Transcript 1 has clear 'exploratory' features. (Examples of talk relating to all three categories can be found in Fisher, 1993; Mercer, 1995; and Wegerif & Mercer, 1996.)

Talk that resembles any of these three types may be appropriate in some social situations. I am not suggesting that any one is good and another is bad. But I think we can make judgements about the educational value of any observed talk in context. And when we do, the analytic category of exploratory talk has a special educational significance. It typifies language which embodies certain principles – of accountability, of clarity, of constructive criticism and receptiveness to well-argued proposals – which are valued highly in many societies.

In my research – and in my own teaching – I have found that students respond well to activities which help them become more aware of how talk is used for joint intellectual activity, and of the ground rules which govern educational discourse. They often seem quite relieved that at last someone is telling them what they are expected to do, and to explain why it is worth doing. Moreover, the amount of exploratory talk which takes place in group work can be increased quite dramatically through the use of specially-designed activities (Dawes *et al.*, 1992; Mercer, 1995, Chapter 6); and children who have explicitly examined and practised exploratory talk with their teacher are significantly better at doing reasoning tasks together than their peers who have not had such experiences (Wegerif & Mercer, 1996).

Conclusion

Embedded in what is written above are my own views on what issues should guide future applied research on language and education. On a theoretical level, I feel that an applied approach to the study of language in education must take more account of:

(a) the historical, cumulative, contextualized nature of all discourse;

(b) the ways language is used as a social mode of thinking, and for guiding the construction of knowledge; and

(c) the nature of education as a process of linguistic socialization.

Dealing with these things will necessarily involve the development of better methods for analysing continuous discourse. But I believe that this development has already begun. For example, the emergence of computer-based corpus analysis methods has much to offer discourse analysts, and there is a growing willingness to bridge the conventional gulf between 'qualitative' and 'quantitative' methodologies and methods (Mercer, forthcoming).

There are also some fairly obvious practical educational implications in what I have said, and which I draw from other classroom-based research as well as my own. First, teachers need to attend to their effectiveness in creating continuity and coherence in their students' educational experience. Second, teachers should give careful, critical consideration to how they 'scaffold' their students' active participation in educated discourse. They should deal explicitly with the nature and functions of different kinds of talk; but they should also give students opportunities to become active, independent users of 'educated' forms of discourse. This means that students must have opportunities to work together in appropriate activities without constant teacher intervention and control. A well-organized programme of study would balance these elements, and I do not think any of the implications I have drawn are particularly controversial. But it would be difficult to find many classrooms today, anywhere in the world, where such ideas are being put systematically into practice.

References

Austin, J. (1962) *How to Do Things with Words.* Oxford: Oxford University Press.
Barton, D. (1994) *Literacy: An introduction to the ecology of written language.* Oxford: Blackwell.
Barnes, D. and Todd, F. (1977) *Communication and Learning in Small Groups.* London: Routledge and Kegan Paul.
—(1995) *Communication and Learning Revisited.* Portsmouth, New Hampshire: Boynton/Cook.
Bhatia, V. (1993) *Analysing Genre: Language in professional settings.* London: Longman.
Bloch, M. (1993) The uses of schooling and literacy in a Zafimaniry village. In B. Street (ed.) *Cross-Cultural Approaches to Literacy.* Cambridge: Cambridge University Press.
Brooks, G., Latham, J. and Rex, A. (1986) *Developing Oral Skills.* London: Heinemann.
Bruner, J. (1985) Vygotsky: A historical and conceptual perspective. In J. Wertsch (ed.) *Culture, Communication and Cognition: Vygotskian perspectives.* Cambridge: Cambridge University Press.
Christie, F. (1984) Young children's writing development: The relationship of writing genres to curriculum genres. In B. Bartlett and J. Carr (eds) *The 1984 Language in Education Conference: A report of proceedings.* Brisbane: Brisbane CAE, 41–69.
Dawes, L. (1995) Team talk. *Junior Education,* March 1995, 26–7.
Dawes, L., Fisher, E. and Mercer, N. (1992) The quality of talk at the computer. *Language and Learning,* October 1992, 22–5.
Dillon, J. T. (1988) *Questioning and Teaching: A manual of practice.* London: Croom Helm.
Drew, P. and Heritage, J. (1992) *Talk at Work: Interaction in institutional settings.* Cambridge: Cambridge University Press.
Edwards, D. and Mercer, N. (1987) *Common Knowledge: The development of understanding in the classroom.* Milton Keynes: Open University Press.
Fisher, E. (1993) Distinctive features of pupil–pupil talk and their relationship to learning. *Language and Education* 7(4), 239–58.
Galton, M., Simon, B. and Croll, P. (1982) *Inside the Primary Classroom.* London: Routledge & Kegan Paul.
Galton, M. and Williamson, J. (1992) *Group Work in the Primary Classroom.* London: Routledge.
Heath, S. B. (1983) *Ways with Words.* Cambridge: Cambridge University Press.
Lemke, J. L. (1990) *Talking Science: Language learning and values.* Norwood, New Jersey: Ablex.
Leont'ev, A. N. (1981) *Problems of the Development of Mind.* Moscow: Progress Publishers.
Maybin, J. (1994) Children's voices: Talk, knowledge and identity. In D. Graddol, J. Maybin and B. Stierer (eds) *Researching Language and Literacy in Social Context* (pp. 131–50). Clevedon: Multilingual Matters.
Mercer, N. (1994) The quality of talk in children's joint activity at the computer. *Journal of Computer Assisted Learning* 10, 24–32.
— (1995) *The Guided Construction of Knowledge: Talk amongst teachers and learners.* Clevedon: Multilingual Matters.

— (forthcoming) Socio-cultural perspectives and the study of classroom discourse. To appear in C. Coll (ed.) *Classroom Discourse*. Madrid: Infancia y Aprendizaje.

Newman, D., Griffin, P. and Cole, M. (1989) *The Construction Zone*. Cambridge: Cambridge University Press.

Open University (1991a) Videocassette 2, *EH232 Computers and Learning*. Milton Keynes: The Open University.

— (1991b) *Talk and Learning 5–16: An in-service pack on oracy for teachers*. Milton Keynes: The Open University.

Rogoff, B. (1990) *Apprenticeship in Thinking*. New York: Oxford University Press.

Rojas-Drummond, S., Mercer, N., Weber, E. and Barocio, R. (1995) Classroom interaction and the development of problem-solving in five year-olds. Paper presented at the Conference of the European Association for Research on Learning and Instruction, Nijmegen, Holland.

Schegloff, E., Sacks, H. and Jefferson, G. (1977) A simplest systematics for the organization for repair in conversation. *Language* 53, 361–82.

Sheeran, Y. and Barnes, D. (1991) *School Writing: Discovering the ground rules*. Buckingham: Open University Press.

Sinclair, J. and Coulthard, M. (1975) *Towards an Analysis of Discourse*. Oxford: Oxford University Press.

Street, B. (1984) *Literacy in Theory and Practice*. Cambridge: Cambridge University Press.

Swales, J. M. (1990) *Genre Analysis: English in academic and research settings*. Cambridge. Cambridge University Press.

Vygotsky, L. (1978) *Mind in Society*. London: Harvard University Press.

Wegerif, R. and Mercer, N. (1996) Computers and reasoning through talk in the classroom. *Language and Education* 10(1), 47–64.

Westgate, D. and Corden, R. (1993) 'What we thought about things': expectations, context and small group talk. *Language and Education* 7(2), 115–22.

Wood, D. (1988) *How Children Think and Learn*. Oxford: Blackwell.

— (1992) Teaching talk. In K. Norman (ed.) *Thinking Voices: The work of the National Oracy Project*. London: Hodder & Stoughton, 197–205.

4 Language Policy and Language Practice in Education

JENNY CHESHIRE
Queen Mary and Westfield College, University of London

Introduction

BAAL's invitation to consider policy issues in education from a sociolinguistic perspective has been an instructive experience for me. Forced to examine educational policies in the two European situations that I know best – England and Switzerland – I realized that although these countries could hardly be more different in their social, political and cultural backgrounds, in each one there is a gap between the language policies that are in place in schools and the language practices that have been documented by sociolinguists. In this paper I will briefly consider some of the reasons why our knowledge and insights have been ignored, and will then suggest some steps that applied linguists could consider taking in order to ensure that our our discipline functions as an applied one in more than name alone.

Language Policy in England and Wales

Standard English has become an important issue in education here, with the implementation of the National Curriculum for English in England and Wales (DFE & Welsh Office, 1995). The National Curriculum states as the requirements for Speaking and Listening at Key Stages 3 and 4, which cover the years between eleven and sixteen, that pupils 'should be … confident users of standard English in formal and informal situations' (DFE & Welsh Office, 1995: 18). I would certainly not dispute the right of all children to learn to become confident users of standard English in writing. However to imagine that all children could

41

achieve this goal for speaking is to completely disregard a large body of research which documents the ways in which our language expresses different aspects of our social and individual identity, and the complex ways in which we use variable features of language to define the context. A blanket educational policy which simply calls for the use of standard English in both formal and informal situations ignores the complex ways in which speakers deploy standard and non-standard features in discourse; and since the use of non-standard English is correlated with socio-economic class, the policy embodied in the National Curriculum for English simply reinforces and institutionalises unequal access to educational achievement.

The National Curriculum for English also takes no account of a recurrent finding in sociolinguistic research, whereby children aged between 11 and 16 – in other words, pupils at Key Stages 3 and 4 – often use non-standard grammatical features more frequently than other age groups. Take the example of multiple negation (as in *she doesn't want nothing*). The research of Wolfram & Fasold in Detroit (1974: 91) showed how children of all social classes use a higher frequency of multiple negation than adults from the same class, including members of the higher socio-economic groups where the adults may use only standard English variants. Similar examples could be given for other grammatical variables (and phonological variables), not simply for English in the many countries where it is spoken, but for other languages also (see Cheshire, 1987: 762).

National policy in England, then, takes no account of the fact that the ages at which schoolchildren are required to use standard English are precisely the ages at which they often seem least inclined to do so. The gap between policy and sociolinguistic practice means that teachers are left to implement an educational policy which contradicts the practice of their pupils. Again we see that insisting on the use of spoken standard English at an age when pupils are developing their social and personal identities reinforces existing inequalities of opportunity: as the example of multiple negation shows (Wolfram & Fasold, 1974), it is the children from the lower socioeconomic groups who use the nonstandard variant with the highest frequency, and whom our educational language policy requires to adapt the most.

Language Policy in Switzerland

For British politicians, most of whom see multilingualism as a problem, Switzerland must be an anomaly. It has the highest income per capita in Europe and the lowest crime rate, yet it is officially multilingual, with four national languages, three of which are currently official (German, French and Italian). The fourth national language, Rumantsch, seems set to become the fourth official language in 1996, when this proposition will be put to the vote. The size of the different language groups is shown in Figure 1 (the 'other' languages are the languages spoken by foreign workers or immigrants and include English, Portuguese and Turkish).

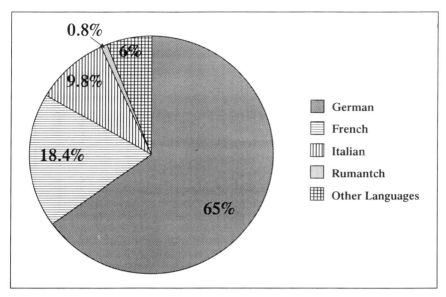

Figure 1 Percentage of the Swiss population belonging to different language groups (from Dürmüller, 1991)

This apparent multilingual paradise does have problems, however. I will focus here on a problem concerning educational language policy in the French-speaking part of the country.

In order to understand Swiss educational language policy it is necessary to know that the overall national language policy rests on two principles. The first is the *principle of individual choice,* which enshrines in law the right of every Swiss citizen to use whichever one of the official languages they prefer. The law states that this right can be exercised when dealing with the federal administration, but in practice the principle is adhered to in many other domains also. The second is the *principle of territoriality*, which gives every Swiss canton the right to decide on the language that will be the official one within that canton. There are four cantons that are bilingual in French and German, but the rest are monolingual. These two principles place an immense burden on the education system, for if the Swiss are to be able to exercise the principle of individual choice when they communicate, school children must learn some of the other

Swiss languages. National policy in Switzerland aims to achieve this through the Partner language model, as set out in Figure 2. The linguistic situation in Switzerland is discussed in more detail in Stevenson (1989) and Pap (1990).

	German speakers	French speakers	Italian speaker	Rumantch speakers
L1	German	French	Italian	Rumantch
L2	French	German	French	German
L3	Italian or English	Italian or English	German	French

Figure 2 The Partner Language Model

National policy in Switzerland, then, aims to construct the Swiss national identity as multilingual and multicultural – a national identity that could hardly be more different from the one which national policy aims to construct for the people of England. Nevertheless, a gap exists between language policy and sociolinguistic practice in Switzerland, just as it does in England. As Figure 2 shows, French-speaking pupils learn German as their second language. The model of German that is used in the schools is standard (High) German, and the textbooks, video materials and audio tapes are all in this variety. Something all sociolinguists know, however, is that German-speaking Switzerland has long been renowned as a classic example of diglossia, a term now seen as an abstraction but originally coined by Ferguson (1959) to refer to societies where two varieties of a language are in complementary distribution, with no overlap in the functions for which they are used. The High variety (High German in the case of Switzerland) is used in writing, in education, on radio and television and in most public speech events, and has to be learned at school; the Low variety (in Switzerland the range of Swiss German dialects) is used in informal speech and is the variety that is acquired at home.

Ferguson's view was that diglossic communities were linguistically stable, since the complementary social functions of the two varieties would work against language shift. He was, we now know, wrong. In Switzerland the dialects are leaking into domains that were previously occupied by High German: they are used in some cantonal parliaments, in secondary schools and some university teaching, and they are heard on radio and television, with a frequency that has been increasing during the last 30 years. Pap (1990) reports that 35 percent of radio and television programmes were in dialect in 1970, but that by 1979 the proportion had risen to 50 percent and by 1988 to 67 percent. The changing diglossic situation in German-speaking Switzerland is discussed in more detail in Watts (1988) and Lee (1992).

Not only are the dialects increasingly used within German-speaking Switzerland, but the Swiss speakers of German are becoming less willing to use High German to communicate with their French-speaking compatriots, preferring to use French, if they can, or English (Dürmüller, 1992; Cheshire & Moser, 1995). The other language groups, therefore, now have little motivation for learning German at school, for they cannot use it to understand the German-speaking Swiss, nor can they reinforce their second language learning by listening to radio or television. Here too, then, there is a gap between policy and practice. Federal policy in Switzerland aims to achieve national unity in the face of diversity by imposing the Partner Language Model, but the model does not take proper account of sociolinguistic practice.

Sociolinguists, Politicians and Journalists

If language policy is out of step with sociolinguistic practice, as in the examples I have discussed here, it is unlikely to achieve its stated aims. The gap between policy and practice could have been avoided if sociolinguists had, as a body, directly engaged with the social and political issues, and it is instructive, therefore, to consider why they did not. I would suggest that one of the main reasons is that politicians and sociolinguists have different agendas.

The agenda of politicians is to execute a predetermined policy. In the case of the National Curriculum for English in England and Wales it is clear from the discussion in Cox (1991) that the Conservative Party politicians had decided on their objectives even before the advisory work on the National Curriculum for English had begun: their aims were for all children to speak and write standard English, and for a return to traditional methods of teaching grammar and spelling. When it became clear that the Cox Committee's recommendations (DES, 1989) did not coincide with the politicians' aims, the politicians simply filtered the recommendations out of the report and excluded the Committee from important decision-making meetings and press conferences.

In the case of Switzerland, politicians aim to construct a multilingual and multicultural national identity for Swiss citizens. Meeting this agenda is difficult at present, however, for national identity is currently a problematic concept for the Swiss. Steinberg (1976) writes that the three largest language groups in Switzerland have always been held together less by what they have in common with each other than by their shared desire to distance themselves from their neighbouring countries. This presumably explains, in part at least, the increasing use of dialect by the German-speaking Swiss, who are thereby able to distance themselves linguistically from Germany. Steinberg's view is that the Swiss have been at their most united during external threats to their country, such as during the Second World War, or during the 'Cold War' period. When there are no external threats, the Swiss focus on their internal divisions. These have been clearly revealed in some of the recent national referenda: in 1992, for example, when the Swiss voted on joining the European Economic Area, each of the French-speaking cantons voted in favour of joining but they were outvoted by the numerically dominant German-speaking cantons. This did not endear the German speakers to the French speakers, for whom the consequences of the economic recession (albeit slight relative to other countries) are causing more hardship than in the economically dominant German-speaking cantons. The younger French-speaking Swiss seem to be turning to English as a way of the expressing linguistically their national identity, preferring this to the problems of using German (Cheshire & Moser, 1995). This, however, is unacceptable to Swiss politicians, who may well recognise the importance of English as an international language but who certainly do not see English as a way of constructing Swiss national identity.

As academics we have a different agenda, trying to understand the sociolinguistic phenomena that we observe. In Switzerland, sociolinguists have analysed the increasing use of English in many different domains of life, and considered the implications for the status of English as a second language or a foreign language (Dürmüller, 1992). Cheshire & Moser (1995) consider the use of English in Switzerland in relation to theories of language display or social identity. In England and Wales, applied linguists responded to a Report of an earlier Advisory Committee on language, the Kingman Committee, with ideological critique, focusing on the Report's gaps, omissions and hidden agendas rather than engaging with the linguistic technicalities of the report (Rampton, 1995: 251). Rampton draws attention to the positive implications of this response, but it is important to remember the negative implications also – in England and Wales, just as in Switzerland, our academic responses have done little to bridge the gap between official educational language policy and sociolinguistic practice.

In both national situations the gap has been filled by a third group of professionals, who again have been pursuing their own objectives. This group consists of journalists, who need to write entertaining copy in order to compete for limited space in their papers. Their efforts to present stories that will grab the reader's attention result in distortions, especially in the tabloid press (Haslam & Bryman, 1994: 191; Gillie, 1994: 181). Bell (1991) has shown how journalists' stories reflect a set of values destined to enhance newsworthiness, with conflict between people, political parties or nations being a staple of news. Similarly, van Dijk (1988) demonstrates the way in which journalists' stories satisfy a rhetoric of emotion and present events in a way that conforms to a favourite ideological script.

L'anglais, langue nationale

de C. et V. PILLONEL
DUILLIER

(…) La langue est un facteur primordial d'unification d'un pays. Malgré cette figure d'Epinal sur les supposés avantages de la diversité des langues et des cultures de la Suisse, il n'en reste pas moins que la plupart des décisions de portée nationale sont prises outre-Sarine. (…)

Ne pas parler couramment la langue de la majorité est un facteur décisif d'exclusion. Allons-nous alors demander aux Romands et aux quelques Tessinois et Romanches qui ne parlent encore que leur langue maternelle de se germaniser pour pouvoir communiquer avec les Alémaniques sur un pied d'égalité?

Non, cela n'est pas possible. Les Romands ne pourront jamais communiquer avec les Alémaniques en essayant de parler le Hochdeutsch. Les Alémaniques communiquent entre eux en Schwyzertütsch et on ne va pas demander aux Romands d'apprendre le ou les Schwyzertütsch. (…)

En conséquence, je propose que l'anglais soit adopté comme langue nationale avec liberté totale pour les étudiants de choisir la langue étrangère qu'ils preferent. Je suppose que cela serait l'anglais la plupart du temps. (…)

L'anglais offre la possibilité de multiples contacts entre toutes les régions du pays et naturellement aussi avec le monde extérieur (…). L'adoption de l'anglais comme langue nationale serait incontestablement un enrichissement culturel et économique et forgerait l'unité de la Suisse.

Figure 3 Extracts from *Le Nouveau Quotidien* 14th March 1995

Figure 3 shows how one of the 'quality' newspapers in French-speaking Switzerland presented the linguistic situation that I described earlier. The story conforms to the values that I have just mentioned. The first paragraph complains that despite the supposed advantages of being a multilingual and multicultural country, for French speakers this means that they are in fact dominated by the more powerful German speakers on the other side of the river Sarine. The following two paragraphs complain about the difficulties of being able to communicate with their German-speaking compatriots on an equal linguistic footing, and the article goes on to propose that Switzerland should therefore adopt English as its national language. In fact. Dürmüller's research (1991) shows that the Swiss are not in favour of adopting English as a national language. The newspaper article demonstrates clearly that while linguists stay silent we leave the way open for journalists to jump into the gap between language policy and sociolinguistic practice, playing on the rhetoric of emotion and fuelling a situation that is already fraught. The result in Switzerland is that policy makers are likely to become still more firmly convinced that they must stick to their policies, averting the potential use of English as a lingua franca in the interests of national unity.

In England and Wales the press exploit tensions between politicians' views and academics' views in a similar way (see, for a good example of this, the discussion in Graddol & Swann (1988). The extract below is just one brief illustration of the way that the popular press seized on the hint of conflict between politicians and academics that was evident after the publication of the Cox Report, belittling experts as 'trendy' and stressing the conflict between politicians and academics:

THATCHER IS FURIOUS WITH 'TRENDY' EXPERTS

A report telling schools to ignore traditional teaching in favour of trendy methods has infuriated Mrs. Thatcher. (Extract from British newspaper quoted by Cox, 1991)

Bridging the Gap

The comparison between Switzerland and England and Wales is useful because it shows that some of the reasons for the gap between policy and practice transcend the specific sociocultural contexts in which the policies and practices are embedded. I have suggested that these reasons include the different agendas held by politicians, journalists and academics, which means that academics tend not to engage directly with policy issues.

Applied linguists, however, are a special kind of academic who, since the 1980s at least, have seen their discipline as one that is specifically concerned with the 'theoretical and empirical study of real-world problems in which language is a central factor' (Brumfit, 1991: 46). I would suggest that we should not stop at the theoretical and empirical study of social problems, and that as an applied discipline we should use our professional expertise to try to solve the real-world problems that we identify. I conclude, therefore, by suggesting some objectives that applied linguists would need to adopt if we are to attempt to bridge the gap between language policies and sociolinguistic practice.

(1) We should engage as a body with specific language issues (such as those that were discussed by the Kingman Committee and the Cox Committee), giving our support to those individual applied linguists who are actually working

with politicians. Confidentiality requirements may prevent us from commenting on details, but the public support of a professional body of linguists may mean that in future linguists appointed to such Committees are less isolated. (See for example Henry Widdowson's experience as a member of the Kingman Committee, which resulted in submission of a dissident minority report: DES, 1988; Rampton, 1995: 251.)

(2) We should work towards raising the level of public knowledge about language. We need to consider how to inform the powerful middle-class sector, for experience has shown that for changes to be made to existing language policies the support of a powerful pressure group is essential: witness, for example, Maori in New Zealand, French in Quebec or Welsh in Wales. In the examples I have discussed in this paper the sociolinguistic practices that are out of step with language policies are those of minority groups (by minority I mean relatively powerless – the French speakers in Switzerland, and speakers of non-standard English in England and Wales).

(3) We need to turn our attention to the question of the representation of language issues in the media. One problem is how to have language issues represented at all; another is how to ensure, if they are represented, that selective gatekeeping does not result in partial news coverage (Ussher 1994) or even in the perpetuation of social problems (Dunning 1994). This is a crucial objective, since our ability to obtain the support of a powerful pressure group and the interest and sympathy of the wider public will depend on our being heard appropriately in the media.

(4) In order to combat the growing disdain with which our expertise is treated (see Rampton 1995), we need to take full account of the ideological positions of those with whom we are obliged to work, taking care not to antagonise more than is necessary the politicians whose support we need but whose opinions we may not share.

(5) Finally, none of the previous objectives will be possible unless they are recognised within our discipline as appropriate for an applied field. In Britain, academics have an agenda that has been imposed on us: our research output is regularly evaluated, by our peers, and our personal promotion prospects as well as the prospects for our department hinge on this evaluation. This, together with the many other tasks we have to do as academics, militates against the possibility of our directly affecting language policies, for we are obliged to publish in scholarly journals, which have a small, closed readership – in effect, we are writing for each other, rather than the world at large. Perhaps we should try to ensure that the Research Assessment Exercise evaluates not only our scholarly writing but also newspaper articles and other kinds of media work. In this case the criteria would be their effectiveness and

their likelihood of contributing to the education of the public on language issues and knowledge about language.

Stubbs (1989: 249) concludes an article in which he sets the Cox Report within its political and cultural context by asking: 'What would happen if people in Britain were just a little less profoundly monolingual, a little more knowledge-able about language diversity and able to discuss it a little more rationally?' I will conclude this article by asking a similar question: what would happen if Associations of Applied Linguistics throughout the world accepted at least some of the objectives I have outlined above? If we all applied our expertise to the question of how to achieve these objectives, we would take an important step towards bridging the gap between language policy and sociolinguistic practice, and towards making our discipline a truly applied one.

References

Bell, A. (1991) *The Language of the News Media.* Oxford: Blackwell.
Brumfit, C. (1991) Applied linguistics in higher education: Riding the storm. *BAAL Newsletter* 38, 45–9.
Cheshire, J. (1987) Age and generation-specific use of language. In V. Ammon, N. Dittmar and K. J. Mattheier (eds) *Sociolinguistics: An international handbook of the science of language and society* (pp. 760–7). Berlin: Walter de Gruyter.
Cheshire, J. and Moser, L.-M. (1995) English and symbolic meaning: Advertisements in the Suisse Romande. *Journal of Multilingual and Multicultural Development* 17, 451–69.
Cox , B. (1991) *Cox on Cox: An English curriculum for the 1990s.* London: Hodder and Stoughton.
DES (1988) *Report of the Committee of Inquiry into the Teaching of the English Language* (The Kingman Report). London: HMSO.
— (1989) *English for Ages 5–16* (The Cox Report). London: DES & Welsh Office.
DFE and Welsh Office (1995) *English in the National Curriculum.* London: HMSO.
Dunning, E. (1994) The sociologist as media football: Reminscences and preliminary reflections. In C. Haslam and A. Bryman (eds) *Social Scientists Meet the Media* (pp. 51–64). London: Routledge.
Dürmüller, D. (1991) Swiss multilingualism and intranational communication. *Sociolinguistica* 5, 111–59.
— (1992) The changing status of English in Switzerland. In V. Ammon and M. Hellinger (eds) *Status Change in Languages* (pp. 355–70). Berlin: Walter de Gruyter.
Ferguson, C. (1959) Diglossia. *Word* 15, 325–40.
Gillie, O. (1994) From science to journalism. In C. Haslam and A. Bryman (eds) *Social Scientists Meet the Media* (pp. 175–85). London: Routledge.
Graddol, D. and Swann, J. (1988) Trapping linguists: An analysis of linguists' responses to John Honey's pamphlet 'The Language Trap'. *Language and Education* 2, 95–112.
Haslam, C. and Bryman, A. (1994) Social scientists and the media: An overview. In C. Haslam and A. Bryman (eds) *Social Scientists Meet the Media* (pp. 186–211). London: Routledge.
Lee, D. (1992) *Competing Discourses: Perspective and ideology in language.* Harlow: Longman.

Pap, P. (1990) The language situation in Switzerland: an updated survey. *Lingua* 80, 109–48.

Rampton, B. (1995) Politics and change in research in applied linguistics. *Applied Linguistics* 16, 233–56.

Steinberg, J. (1976) *Why Switzerland?* Cambridge: Cambridge University Press.

Stevenson, P. (1989) Political culture and intergroup relations in plurilingual Switzerland. *Journal of Multilingual and Multicultural Development* 11, 227–55.

Stubbs, M. (1989) The state of English in the English state: Reflections on the Cox Report. *Language and Education* 3, 235–50.

Ussher, J. (1994) Media representations of psychology: Denigration and popularization, or worthy dissemination of knowledge? In C. Haslam and A. Bryman (eds) *Social Scientists Meet the Media* (pp. 123–37). London: Routledge.

van Dijk, T. (1988) *News as Discourse.* New York: Lawrence Erlbaum.

Watts, R. (1988) Language, dialect and national identity in Switzerland. *Multilingua* 7, 313–34.

Wolfram, W. and Fasold, R. (1974) *The Study of Social Dialects in American Speech.* Englewood Cliffs, NJ: Prentice Hall.

5 Multilingualism and Education: The case of Ethiopia

THOMAS BLOOR and WONDWOSEN TAMRAT
Aston University and *Kotobe College of Teacher Education*

Multilingualism and Progressive Politics

It is a truism of current Western liberal thinking that all languages are deserving of respect and that ethnic preferences with regard to language should be encouraged. The suppression of minority languages in the interests of national unity has for some time been identified with right-wing authoritarianism. In a discussion of Spanish language policy, Mar-Molinero (1990) comments: 'Besides proscribing the use of such local languages as Catalan, Basque and Galician, the Franco regime also set out to downgrade their prestige' (1990: 52).

Phillipson points out that 'the legal measures designed to buttress French closely resemble those of Fascist regimes (Italy, Germany, Spain)' (1992: 106). The campaign for an official English-Only policy in the United States is strongly identified with the political Right. The history of English as a world language is clearly related to its status as the language of British colonialism and, more recently, US neo-colonialism. Indeed, the expansion of English has been a particular target for criticism from progressives.

A corollary of liberal respect for multilingualism is the view that every individual is entitled to education in his or her mother tongue. This right – or its desirability in principle – is enshrined in various publications of the United Nations and its satellite organizations (for example, UNESCO, 1953).

It has not been ever thus. The French Revolution made no concessions to linguistic minorities but increased the hegemony of Metropolitan, even Parisian,

French. (Perhaps this is not surprising in what some scholars see as the start of the modern nation state.) That great liberal cause, Italian unification, incorporated a commitment to forging a national standard language at the expense of significantly differing dialects – or regional languages – as did the unification of Germany. In the years of mass European immigration into the 'melting pot' of the United States, integration via the unifying force of the English language was widely perceived as a thoroughly liberal goal (though it is now easy to find contrary views of the American language requirements in the nineteenth and early twentieth century, for example, in Baron, 1990).

Taylor observes:

> Until the early 1960s, in the United States, and to some extent, Canada, politicians and public alike, supported by theory in the social sciences, envisaged a single outcome to the integration process – assimilation. (1991: 1)

More recently, the oppressive apartheid government of the Republic of South Africa consistently demoted English. This was done not only to promote Afrikaans, the language of the ruling minority, but also to encourage the use of so-called 'tribal' languages: Setswana, Sesotho, Khosa, Zulu, etc., in pursuit of a divide-and-rule policy and effective censorship of reading matter. The commitment to English of the African National Congress and other anti-government organizations (such as the Unity Movement and the Communist Party) during the period of struggle was an outcome of their clear recognition of the reactionary nature of the government's language policy and its potentially detrimental effects on African unity in the battle against apartheid (Eastman, 1991; Bloor & Bloor, 1990). None of this is to deny the colonial legacy of early British domination or the fact that English was the language of many members of the oppressive minority in South Africa, including the predominantly wealthier elements.

Thus it can be seen that, whilst it is certainly the case that a commitment to multilingualism is identifiable with progressive politics in many – perhaps most – instances, it is not so intrinsically and in all circumstances. As with most issues, the complexities of the context must be taken into account. Pennycook posits the question:

> whether, in looking at the relationships between language and inequality, there is not a danger of focusing too much on 'linguistic imperialism' and expansionism, rather than trying to understand the implications of both insistence on and denial of a language within larger structures of inequality. (1994: 74)

Developments in Ethiopia

Ethiopia has an estimated population of about the same size as Britain, just over 53 million. The number of languages spoken as mother tongues has been variously assessed for the usual reasons: the difficulties of delimiting languages in a dialect continuum, the use of different names for the same language, the use of the same name for different languages, and so on; not to mention the limited national resources for carrying out surveys in this – or, for that matter, any other – field. However, respectable recent estimates give a figure of 99 distinct languages (Wedekind, 1994). These fall into four family groups: Cushitic, Semitic, Omotic (all of these groups being Afro-Asiatic languages) and a cluster of Nilo-Saharan languages with a small number of speakers, dwelling for the most part close to the Sudan border. According to very dated estimates (Bender *et al.*, 1976), there are probably more speakers of Semitic than Cushitic languages, but each accounts for well over 40% of the population, whilst Omotic languages represent only about 5%. The main representatives of Cushitic and Semitic respectively are Orominya and Amharinya (or Oromo and Amharic). Recent official estimates give Oromo speakers as 29.1% of the population and Amharic speakers as 28.3%. The third most populous language is the Semitic language Tigrinya with 9.7%. There is an extensive and sophisticated literature in Amharic and Tigrinya dating back for centuries.

Eastman (1991: 137) includes Ethiopia (along with Kenya, Nigeria and Zaire) as representing the most multilingual situation, namely Laitin's (1989) 3 +/- 1 category, i.e. where people know two to four languages. According to Eastman, the four are: a first language, a vernacular used in primary education, a lingua franca, and a colonial language. In fact, although the numerical formula is probably about right, Eastman's designation of the languages making up the four is not accurate for Ethiopia, not least because Ethiopia is the sole African country to have escaped European colonization.

For several centuries until 1975 (with a short interval of Italian invasion and military occupation from 1935 to 1941), Ethiopia consisted of a turbulent amalgamation of territories (kingdoms and, later, provinces) under the feudal rule of an emperor (*negus negast*, literally king of kings). All the emperors were speakers of Amharic except for one Tigrinya speaker in the nineteenth century. As a result Amharic became established as the language of the imperial court, the law-courts and the capital city and eventually as the official language of the state.

The dominant religion, Coptic (Ethiopian Orthodox) Christianity, has tended to reinforce the spread of Amharic for, although the liturgical language is Gi'iz, an otherwise defunct Semitic language, the language of much church activity is Amharic; furthermore, the last emperor, Haile Selassie, permitted Protestant and

Roman Catholic missionaries to proselytise only via the medium of Amharic and only in non-Christian areas. Literacy in Amharic, as well as Gi'iz scholarship, was developed largely through the traditional church schools.

Under the long autocratic reign of Haile Selassie, whose explicit aim was to modernize the country, a non-fee-paying state education system was developed. Although the monarch's own education was in French, the predominant pattern from 1947 was English-medium with Amharic as a taught subject. In 1958, a hasty programme of Amharicization was initiated, reversing the roles of Amharic and English in elementary school, but with English remaining the medium for secondary and tertiary education. Rudimentary adult literacy programmes were also in Amharic, and in public speeches the Emperor promoted Amharic as the national language. In daily life, and minimally in such activities as the law (litigation being endemic to Ethiopia), some concessions were made to other indigenous languages, but in the education system they were largely ignored.

In 1973, Haile Selassie was overthrown by a military junta, the Derg (literally: the Committee), who paid lip-service to some recognition of vernaculars (i.e. indigenous languages other than Amharic). For example, the Derg initiated the extensive vernacular literacy programme (according to Cooper, 1989) as a device for scattering the increasingly restive student population, but this was a hopeless failure. Cooper, writing while the Derg remained in power, reports:

> while the Ministry of Education briefly considered the possibility of using local languages as the vehicle of instruction in elementary school, the Emperor's policy of Amharicization has been continued. (1989: 28)

In the state system under the Derg, the medium throughout primary education (six years) was Amharic and in secondary school it was English. English was also taught as a subject in primary school.

The outcome of the prolonged and bloody civil war of the 1970s and 80s was the destruction of the Derg and its replacement by the Ethiopian People's Revolutionary Democratic Front. This represents itself as an amalgamation of several revolutionary ethnic parties, speaking for all ethnic groupings; it includes, among others, very influential Tigrinya speakers from the former Tigray Liberation Front.

For the first time, Ethiopia's leaders are showing a very strong commitment to status planning which is geared to the recognition and development of indigenous living languages other than Amharic. The policy which they have selected is a territorial one, akin in some ways to the model of Belgium or Canada. However, there is a major difference: whereas the division in these countries is binary or ternary, Ethiopia has established nine linguistic regions.

The vernacular (that is, the officially designated language of the region) is upgraded at the expense of Amharic in a number of domains, notably in the judiciary, district and regional administration, and place of worship, where the intention is that it will entirely replace Amharic (except, of course, where Amharic is the designated regional language). Amharic, which remains the national language, will still dominate the mass media but with more time being given than previously to vernacular broadcasting and newspaper publication. The language of central government will remain Amharic. In the new school curriculum, the medium throughout primary school is the vernacular; the medium in secondary school (and beyond) is English. English is taught as a subject throughout primary school (now eight years) and Amharic in upper primary and lower secondary (six years) (Transitional Government of Ethiopia, 1994).

Some Problems

On the face of it, this policy appears optimally to meet the requirements for a modern progressive policy, but there are serious problems. According to recent government estimates, only 20% of the relevant age group attend primary school and many drop out before completion of the primary phase, often after only one or two years. Only 12% attend secondary school. According to a Ministry of Education report (1993) 60% of secondary teachers are inadequately qualified. Primary teachers have always been for the most part very poorly educated. At present, the vast majority of this handicapped teaching force is, within its limits, very largely competent to work through the medium of Amharic though it is unlikely that similar competence exists in the other Ethiopian languages, with the possible exception of Tigrinya.

Ethiopia is a desperately poor country. Even with the old Amharic-medium policy, resources were inadequate. However, there exists a substantial body of pedagogic texts in Amharic and a very considerable exploitation of written Amharic outside the school system, providing the sort of back-up material required for literacy to take hold. There is little or nothing in most of the other languages (except Tigrinya). Cooper attributes the failure of the Derg's mass literacy campaign to a number of factors, one of which is most relevant to our present point:

> Little account was taken of the fact that only in Amharic and Tigrinya were there reading materials – other languages having no written tradition. This would have been a serious bar to the attainment of functional mass literacy, which requires access to useful, everyday written materials if new readers are not to lapse back into illiteracy. (1989:26)

McGroarty *et al.* (1995) point to the lack of linguistic assessment instruments for indigenous languages in the USA, mentioning among other reasons lack of funds. If the USA cannot, or will not, develop adequate materials for minority language speakers, what hope has a poor nation like Ethiopia?

It is perhaps worth while pointing out that, for the foreseeable future, there is no possibility at all of realizing the UNESCO ideal of every individual child having the right to education in his or her mother tongue. To begin with, only a small fraction of the 99 languages spoken will be catered for. Furthermore, even in the unlikely situation of every child getting any sort of education at all, the system does not allow for the accommodation of individual requirements. The vernacular through which the child will be educated will be the vernacular assigned to the region in which she lives. Since the languages in question are by no means geographically discrete, many pupils will find themselves initiated into the educational process via a second language, just as in the Amharic-medium times. It seems that some concessions may be made, rules may be bent, but for the majority it will be location rather than mother tongue that determines the medium of instruction.

In spite of the secondary and tertiary English-medium policy, most educated Ethiopians are far more fluent in Amharic than in English, and Amharic is normally the preferred medium of social discourse in educated multi-vernacular groups. Though by no means the only lingua franca in the country, Amharic is to date by far the most widespread and is used by more people than any other. English is not a contender in this respect except where foreigners are involved. In fact, compared with its status in most so-called Anglophone African countries, English is relatively poorly established outside the education system.

The effect of the new curriculum, however, is to boost English at the expense of Amharic. Whereas in the old curriculum all children in primary school were immersed in the national language and acquired a smattering of English (since for most that was all that the primary curriculum provided), very early drop-outs will not be exposed to Amharic at all in future, and even primary completers will have very little exposure to it.

Contemporary scholars working in the field of language planning bemoan the lack of status of indigenous African languages, which are seen as increasingly losing out to colonial languages, particularly English and French. Breton remarks:

> As far as one can see, more than 30 years since the outset of independence, little has been done for African '*national*' language development, and the position of European '*official*' languages is stronger in sub-Saharan Africa than it has ever been before. (1991: 158)

Ethiopia was a notable exception to this position, a fact not unconnected with its history of freedom from European domination. Of course, there may be understandable resentment among other language groups of the history of Amhara domination. Cooper (1989) reports that some Tigrinya-speaking students in the 1970s refused to speak Amharic, but this was a political act rather than a reflection of any lack of ability to speak the language (compare the militant minority of Welsh speakers who are reluctant to use English). History and ethnic aspirations cannot and should not be ignored, but it would be ironic if the result of this concession to vernacular education should prove to be an extension of the role of English, attacked by scholars such as Phillipson (1992) as the colonial language par excellence. It is perhaps significant that the British Overseas Development Administration has just launched an aid project committed to primary English in Ethiopia. Of course, there is no immediate prospect of English becoming a serious lingua franca; it will remain restricted to a small minority of the population and Amharic will retain some of its former importance, but it will be made accessible to fewer people and literacy might well suffer.

Eastman, commenting on apartheid policy in South Africa, says:

> Amidst all this existed the now controversial MTP or Mother Tongue Policy by which *all* people were to be schooled initially in their first language. Here, as elsewhere on the continent, this led to a situation where those who are poor and unable to go beyond primary grades are cut off linguistically from access to political and economic power. Though conforming to the 1951 UNESCO-mandated goal of first-language literacy, such a policy has had dubious educational benefits for most Bantu speakers, whether in South Africa or East Africa. (1991: 143)

Notwithstanding the very different motivations, malign in the case of the former South Africa, presumably benign in that of Ethiopia, there may be a lesson to be learned from the situation described by Eastman. It would be tragic if the recognition of the legitimate desires and aspirations of citizens should lead to a diminution of their access through education to knowledge and power, just as it would be a disaster for the diversity of world languages if one of the few indigenous African languages with major national status should be forced to give ground to the encroachment of international English.

References

Baron, D. (1990) *The English-Only Question: An official language for Americans?* New Haven and London: Yale University Press.
Bender, M. L., Bowen, J. D., Cooper, R. L. and Ferguson, C. A. (eds) (1976) *Language in Ethiopia.* London: Oxford University Press.
Bloor, M. and Bloor, T. (1990) The role of English in resurgent Africa. In R. Clark, N. Fairclough, R. Ivanic, N. McLeod, J. Thomas and P. Meara (eds) *Language and Power* (pp. 32–43). London: CILT for BAAL.

Breton, R. (1991) The handicap of language planning in Africa. In D. F. Marshall (ed.) *Language Planning: Focusschrift in Honor of Joshua A. Fishman* (pp. 153–74). Amsterdam and Philadelphia: John Benjamins.

Cooper, R. L. (1989) *Language Planning and Social Change*. Cambridge: Cambridge University Press.

Eastman, C. M. (1991) The politics and sociolinguistics of status planning in Africa. In D. F. Marshall (ed.) *Language Planning: Focusschrift in Honor of Joshua A. Fishman* (pp. 135–51). Amsterdam and Philadelphia: John Benjamins.

Laitin, D. D. (1989) A political perspective on language repertoires in Africa. Draft for ASA 1990. Social Science Research Council.

Mar-Molinero, C. (1990) Language policies in post-Franco Spain: Conflict of central goals and local objectives. In R. Clark, N. Fairclough, R. Ivanic, N. McLeod, J. Thomas and P. Meara (eds) *Language and Power* (pp. 52–63). London: CILT for BAAL.

McGroarty, M., Beck, M. and Butler, F. A. (1995) Policy issues in assessing indigenous languages: A Navajo case. *Applied Linguistics* 16/3, 323–43.

Ministry of Education (1993) *Ethiopian Educational Policy Implementation Strategy*. Addis Ababa: Ministry of Education.

Pennycook, A. (1994) *The Cultural Politics of English as an International Language*. London and New York: Longman.

Phillipson, R. (1992) *Linguistic Imperialism*. Oxford: Oxford University Press.

Taylor, D. M. (1991) The social psychology of racial and cultural diversity: Issues of assimilation and multiculturalism. In A. G. Reynolds (ed.) *Bilingualism, Multiculturalism, and Second Language Learning: The McGill Conference in Honour of Wallace E. Lambert* (pp. 1–19). Hillsdale, NJ and London: Lawrence Erlbaum Associates.

Transitional Government of Ethiopia (1994) *Education and Training Policy*. Addis Ababa.

UNESCO (1953) *The Use of Vernacular Languages*. Paris: UNESCO.

Wedekind, K. (1994) Updating linguistic maps. In *Survey of Little-Known Languages, Linguistic Reports No. 13*. Addis Ababa: Institute of Ethiopian Studies/Summer Institute of Linguistics.

6 Outing the Tester: Theoretical models and practical endeavours in language testing

ALAN DAVIES
University of Edinburgh/University of Melbourne

Theoretical Influence: The claim and the reality

The argument of this paper can be explained by reference to the book Geoff Brindley has recently edited: *Language Assessment in Action* (Brindley, 1995). The book brings together 11 case studies of English as a Second Language (ESL) assessment situations in Australia. Brindley shows, in his Introduction and in his selection of papers, that reflection on engagement in the language class has encouraged creative thinking about observation and process; it has also encouraged on the job, performance based integration of teaching and assessment. This integration can provide a focus on 'language as a tool for communication rather than on language knowledge as an end in itself' (Brindley, 1995: 158). What Brindley does not say is that communicative language assessment must, like all assessment, provide clear information about learning success. It is not evident that it does: indeed the information it does provide may confuse because of mismatches of teachers' and learners' expectations.

Brindley makes the following case for the volume:

> the last few years have ... seen greatly increased activity in the development of tests and assessment procedures for assessing, monitoring and reporting learners' proficiency, progress and achievement in ESL programs. These range from large-scale proficiency tests and reporting systems to informal monitoring procedures aimed at assisting teachers to keep track of individual

classroom learning. The aim of this volume is to bring together a range of these testing and assessment initiatives and to document the issues, problems and dilemmas which arise as practitioners and language testers attempt to devise systems, instruments and procedures to meet their particular assessment needs. (1995: 1)

There are, writes Brindley, relatively few case study accounts of the way in which assessment tools have been constructed to meet the needs of particular groups. He hopes that

this volume will fill this gap by providing some insights into the rationales and decision-making processes which have accompanied the development of tests and assessments in both institutional and classroom contexts. (1995: 1)

Does it fill the gap? The topics discussed all attempt solutions to practical problems. They include: the assessment needs of large-scale systems; 'Exrater', a computer program incorporating an 'expert system' aimed at assisting language assessors to apply the Australian Second Language Proficiency Ratings (ASLPR); a task-based instrument for assessing achievement of objectives in an English for Professional Employment course for adult immigrants; criterion-based assessment procedures; self-assessment in language programmes.

Bachman's theoretical volume *Fundamental Considerations in Language Testing* (1990) acts as a start-up *vademecum* for most contributors to this volume: the book appears in nine of the 11 individual lists of references. A relevant question of course is to what extent the authors' conclusions on their assessment experiences support that early appeal to Bachman. There is little evidence either way. True, Mincham concludes that 'focus on a predetermined set of criteria helped (the teachers) in becoming more aware of learners' individual needs' (1995: 87). But Gunn takes a contrary view: 'we discovered only through practice how difficult it is to specify criteria for task performance in a clear and unambiguous way' (1995: 261). My own reading of these contributions does not accord with the strong theoretical tilt Brindley gives in his Introduction. He refers to 'the growing number of test development projects which draw explicitly on current theoretical frameworks of communicative language ability, in particular those proposed by Bachman (1990) and Bachman & Palmer (forthcoming)' (1995: 8).

However, when we examine the actual use of Bachman's model in the projects Brindley presents, there has to be a suspicion of lip-service. For example, in her chapter, McKay moves from this statement:

the ESL Development Project chose to adopt as a theoretical base for the development of the ESL Bandscales (and the assessment and reporting

materials) the Bachman (1990, 1991) and Bachman & Palmer (forthcoming)
framework of communicative language ability (1995: 40)

to:

> A key underlying aim in (Bachman's) approach is to make the construct,
> the underlying ability of second language ability *(sic)* testable. However,
> there are difficulties in this approach ... In effect, the NLLIA ESL Develop-
> ment Project has taken a 'weak' interpretation of the Bachman/Palmer
> framework ... (it) is used as a general guide. (1995: 44)

This reads to me more like claiming to draw explicitly on current theoretical
frameworks than actually doing so.

The volume's somewhat forced yoking of the theoretical and the practical
takes us no nearer the holy grail of true proficiency: what it tells us is that if you
set up a model of language proficiency people will say they are following it,
whether they are or not. While the case studies reported in the volume under
review provide interesting and thoughtful accounts of the realities of engagement in language teaching and testing, they could have done with less applied
model and more applied linguistics.

The Temptation of Self-Reflexivity

The lack of fit is of course not confined to language testers. It has been suggested in linguistic commentaries by Lyons, among others, that it is important to
look at what linguists do rather than at what they say:

> Linguistics, like any other science, builds on the past; and it does so,
> not only by challenging and refuting traditional doctrines, but also by
> developing and reformulating them ... many recent works on linguistics, in
> describing the great advances made in the scientific investigation of lan-
> guage in the last few decades, have neglected to emphasize the continuity
> of Western linguistic theory from earliest times to the present day. (Lyons
> 1971: 3)

In other words, the practice of linguistics does not change very much as opposed
to its theorising. What this suggests is that the writing of grammars and the
description of language systems attract general agreement among professional
linguists.

There are of course two ways of interpreting this judgement. The first is that
our understanding is at fault when we try to interpret the arguments about
linguistics, as representing different positions. If we knew more, (we might
think) we would be able to reach behind the rhetoric to what is really being said
and recognise that the apparent oppositions are not substantial ones.

The second interpretation (or is it an extension of the first?) can be understood as meaning that whether or not there are such theoretical disagreements, what really matters is how linguists go about their linguistic work. If that is what Lyons means (and I suspect it is) then it suggests that for him applications and practice (a particular sort of applied linguistics) are what linguistics is really about.

There is a third interpretation which seems to me highly plausible, and that is that linguists' reflexive theoretical discourse is what really matters in linguistics. In other words, when they disagree (as for example the pro- and anti-Chomskyans do), what they are disagreeing about is not how to do linguistics but what linguistics is. We see this in Harris's comment: 'he's not even doing linguistics anymore', a typical Chomskyan comment on Lakoff, 'as if linguistics was the only way to look at language or, for that matter, as if there was only one way to do linguistics' (Harris, 1993: 246). Certainly you get that sense in others of the social sciences and in English literature and cultural studies. We seem to be observing not so much the politicising of the humanities as their philosophising. I suppose it could be regarded as a necessary academic cleansing exercise to clear the ground before we go on to re-engage with very different primary data.

Communicative Models in Language Testing

In language testing, as in applied linguistics generally, there have been speculation and theoretical discussion over the last 15 years with regard to communicative models. I want to consider briefly two such theoretical models, the communicative model of language testing (Canale & Swain, 1980) and the performance model (Bachman, 1990), itself a development of the Swain and Canale model. I shall then contrast them with a language test in use and with language test constructors' views of how it is they construct language tests.

Canale & Swain (1980) and Canale (1983) proposed a communicative model for second language teaching and testing in which the knowledge component contained grammatical competence, sociolinguistic competence, strategic competence and (later) discourse competence. It was this knowledge component which they termed communicative competence, restricting it to language knowledge. Ability for use they relegate outside the model to communicative performance, which for them meant actual use. They deliberately excluded communicative performance (or ability for use) from their competence model, in part because to include it would have raised the question of deficit. Later writers have pointed out that ability for use is in itself another knowledge component and, interestingly, the one which differentiates among native speakers (Davies, 1991).

The fact is that the binary distinction between competence and performance (or knowledge and skill) is always inadequate because skill requires to look both ways: there is a knowledge skill and a skill skill (or doing skill). In other words, knowledge 'what' can never be clearly distinguished from from knowledge 'how'.

Bachman, building on Canale and Swain, proposes a model of communicative language ability which contains the following components: language competence, strategic competence, psychophysiological mechanisms/skills. So – to simplify – Bachman has two basic competences, a language competence, and a strategic competence. His language competence is broken down into organisational competence and pragmatic competence, while strategic competence represents the ability to use language. This is 'a general ability which enables an individual to make the most effective use of available abilities in carrying out a given task' (Bachman, 1990: 106). Bachman's model, while more elaborate than the Canale and Swain, has also been criticised, for example by Spolsky: 'I am forced to conclude, then, that the model of communicative competence proposed by Canale and Swain is oversimplified, as is the somewhat different three-component model described by Bachman' (Spolsky, 1989: 147).

This debate matters for language testing because it is not new: the knowledge-ability/skill balance is an old problem, reflected in the familiar distinction between accuracy and fluency. What Canale and Swain were reaching towards, and what Bachman has been very up-front about, is that the strategic competence, which Canale and Swain included within knowledge, and which Bachman separated from language (and has now relabelled Metacognitive Strategies), is itself influenced by the testing event. Hence the importance currently given to performance testing (emphasising audience specificity and production, that is speaking and writing) and to sophisticated methods of statistical test analysis (for example item response theory) which attempt to tease out the candidate and situation etc. facets influencing performance.

The Japanese Language Test for Tour Guides

In order to examine what it is language testers actually do (as distinct from what it is they may say they do) when they are engaged in test development, I refer now to an occupation specific performance test developed at the University of Melbourne's Language Testing Research Centre, the Japanese Language Test for Tour Guides (LTRC, 1992). This test is designed to certify the Japanese language skills of non-native Japanese speakers in the Australian tourism industry who wish to seek work as tour guides.

The *Handbook for Candidates* informs us that:

the test measures speaking and listening skills through a series of role plays conducted with a trained assessor. These role plays are based on an analysis of the types of interaction frequently undertaken by tour guides. The test lasts for approximately half an hour, with a 20 minute preparation time. Reading and writing skills are not assessed. (LTRC, 1992)

Two trained assessors take part in the test, which contains a series of role-plays such as: 'Handling difficult situations', 'Presentation of a culture-related topic', 'Giving instructions', 'Describing the itinerary for the day'. In each case the information for the role-play is provided. Here is one example from the 'Handling difficult situations' section:

Role: You are a guide sending off a party of Japanese tourists at the airport. The flight leaves at 5pm.

Issue: You arrive at the airport to find that the flight has been postponed until the next day because of technical problems. Your office has informed you that the group should return to the same hotel, dinner has been arranged and a half-day tour will be organised for tomorrow morning. One member of the group is rather upset at the change. Reassure him/her.

Such an exercise makes a great deal of sense: what is more, it is, like the other role-plays in the test, 'based on an analysis of the types of interaction frequently undertaken by tour guides.' (LTRC, 1992)

What, then, are we to make of the references in the Final Report on the project to recent discussion in the language testing research literature on models of communicative ability, in particular Bachman (1990) and Canale & Swain (1980)? How do we relate the very practical role-play preparation to the theoretical consideration of models:

These models of language proficiency, or communicative language ability, include illocutionary and sociolinguistic knowledge as well as the ability to use communication strategies in actual communicative situations. (Brown, 1992: 14)

What is the relation here between theory and practice? The requirement of any test is that it should allow the candidate's 'true' knowledge and skill to be displayed to their best advantage. In a test such as this Japanese Language Test for Tour Guides one of the major sources of unreliability is that different raters (or assessors) have different characteristics: these need to be taken account of. The empirical test analysis method can help with that. But where does that leave the theorising behind the test? It seems to me that it is essentially in terms of offering an explanation for what is being practised, rather than the preliminary modelling role that might (naively?) have been expected.

Investigating Influences on Language Testers

Now I want to look at what language testers say about their own activity in test development. Here, as in the account of the content of the Japanese Language Test for Tour Guides, we are concerned with the practical activity of testing, as indicated by language testers' perceptions of what they actually do when they are engaged in developing language tests.

I gave a short questionnaire to a number of people engaged in language testing. The questionnaire consists of four questions about the choices made in language test development work. The questions asked about (1) respondents' experience of different types of work within language testing; (2) the importance they (think they) give to the views of different stakeholders; (3) the priority (in their view) of influences on them in their language testing work; and (4) what they think most influences stakeholders in deciding what it is they want.

Results

Of the 65 questionnaires distributed, 27 were returned completed, a 40% return rate which is reckoned to be an acceptable figure for postal surveys of this type.

Question 1 (Results are reported here in raw figures):

Which of these areas of language testing are you/have you been involved in?

construction of new language tests	25
adaptation of existing language tests	13
administration of language tests	25
production of ad hoc classroom language tests	21
teaching language testing	20
research in language testing	23
language testing consultancies	16

25 of the 27 are involved in language test construction. The other choices attracted similar responses for administration, ad hoc classroom tests, teaching and research. Adaptation and consultancies were somewhat lower. We may conclude that the sample has similar and wide-ranging experience in language testing.

Question 2 (Results are reported here as averages: the lower the average, the greater the importance):

Indicate the importance you give to the views of each of the following stakeholders in your language testing work.

1. Language testers   1.6

   ....

2. Applied linguists   2.2
3. Language teachers   2.3
4. Test takers   2.5

   ....

5. Psychometricians   3.2
6. Administrators   3.3
7. Funding bodies   3.5

There were significant gaps between 1/2 and 4/5. Colleagues, 'the profession', have most influence on the work done by language testers. Nos 2, 3 and 4 are very close to one another.

Question 3 (Results are reported here as averages: the lower the average, the greater the importance):

The language tests you use or adapt or construct in your work inevitably sample across the range of possible test types, tasks and methods. List in order of priority the influences on the choices you make among test types, tasks and methods:

1. Practical (e.g. local knowledge, resources, time, money)   1.6
2. Theoretical (e.g. applied linguistics, proficiency models)   1.9

   ....

3. Political (i.e. what is acceptable to local stakeholders)   2.6

   ....

4. Chance (whatever is available at the time)   4.6

There were significant gaps between 2/3 and 3/4. Although practical considerations are most important, theoretical ones follow very closely. Political considerations are next; nothing else matters.

Question 4 (Results are reported here as averages: the lower the average, the greater the importance):

What in your view most influences stakeholders (other than language testers) in their decisions about the kinds of language tests they want?

1. Traditional views about language and tests   2.6
2. Gut feelings about language and tests   2.7

....

3. Washback to language teaching   3.8
4. Their experience of language teaching   4.1
5. Research in language testing   4.5

There was a significant gap here between 2/3. What this suggests is that stakeholders bring their own prejudices and background to the task. Language testers themselves are influenced by their peers, by the practical constraints of the task in hand and by the theoretical models under discussion. This indicates a healthy enough profession. But language testers have a hard task to influence the other stakeholders (particularly the contracting stakeholder) since the only real influences on them are their own prejudices and personal experiences. All the more reason of course for (a) more professionalising of language testers (and applied linguists more generally) in order to have and to be seen to have professional training and professional standards; and (b) clearer information about the professional expertise needed for language test construction (and more generally for doing applied linguistics).

Conclusions

I have revised my own views as a result of this paper. When I began this research I proposed a three-way distinction:

theoretical models → research → practice (test construction)

meaning that theory would inform research, which in its turn would inform practice. That now seems an over-idealised model. What I have concluded after this examination of the Japanese Language Test for Tour Guides and the survey of language testers is that the role of theory is to relate to practice just as much as to research. After all, language testers are, as we have seen, engaged more or less equally in research and practice or test construction: out of the total of 27, 25 are involved in research and 23 in test construction. What theory therefore does is *both* to explain *and* inform research and practice. It is not that research intervenes between theory and practice, rather that theory intervenes between research and practice, explaining and informing both, though of course it is always more likely to inform research than practice. It was naive of me to think otherwise.

References

Bachman, L. F. (1990) *Fundamental Considerations in Language Testing*. Oxford: Oxford University Press.

Bachman, L. F. and Palmer, A. S. (forthcoming) *Language Testing in Practice: Designing and developing useful language tests*. Oxford: Oxford University Press.

Brindley, G. (ed.) (1995) *Language Assessment in Action*. Research Series 8, NCELTR, Macquarie University, Sydney NSW 2109.

Brown, A. (1992) *Final Report: Japanese Language Occupational Proficiency Test Project*. NLLIA, Language Testing Research Centre, University of Melbourne.

Canale, M. (1983) From communicative competence to communicative language pedagogy. In J. C. Richards and R. W. Schmidt (eds) *Language and Communication* (pp. 2–27). London: Longman.

Canale, M. and Swain, M. (1980) Theoretical bases of communicative approaches to second language teaching and testing. *Applied Linguistics* 1/1, 1–47.

Davies, A. (1991) *The Native Speaker in Applied Linguistics*. Edinburgh: Edinburgh University Press.

Gunn, M. (1995) Criterion-based assessment: A classroom teacher's perspective. In G. Brindley (ed.) *Language Assessment in Action* (pp. 239–70). Research Series 8, NCELTR, Macquarie University, Sydney NSW 2109.

Harris, R. A. (1993) *The Linguistics Wars*. New York: Oxford University Press.

LTRC (1992) *The Japanese Language Test for Tour Guides: Handbook for Candidates*. NLLIA, Language Testing Research Centre, University of Melbourne.

Lyons, J. (1971) *Introduction to Theoretical Linguistics*. Cambridge: Cambridge University Press.

McKay, P. (1995) Developing ESL proficiency descriptions for the school context: The NLLIA ESL bandscales. In G. Brindley (ed.) *Language Assessment in Action* (pp. 31–63). Research Series 8, NCELTR, Macquarie University, Sydney NSW 2109.

Mincham, L. (1995) ESL student needs procedures: An approach to language assessment in primary and secondary school contexts. In G. Brindley (ed.) *Language Assessment in Action* (pp. 65–91). Research Series 8, NCELTR, Macquarie University, Sydney NSW 2109.

Spolsky, B. (1989) Competence, proficiency and beyond. *Applied Linguistics* 10/2, 138–56.

7 Discourses of Rationality: Argumentation in EAP and teacher education across cultures

SIMON GIEVE
University of Lancaster

Introduction[1]

This paper is a report of work in progress, a study of Malaysian English Language teachers who are taking a two-year BEd (TESL) course in Britain. It constitutes a consideration of possible theoretical approaches which might allow understanding of elements which have appeared significant in the data.

The group I have been working with is a cohort of 15 experienced English teachers, each of whom had three or four years of teacher training before coming to Britain. Here, they have attended courses in ELT methodology and testing, linguistics, and education, and received study skills training and on-going support.

My initial research question was *What is going on here?* What is it about the nature of their experience in Britain which is salient to them, which is different from teacher training in Malaysia, and which might justify the organisation of a five-year rolling programme training 800 teachers in all? Rather than evaluating the programme by investigating the aims and expectations of the sponsoring agency, the relevance and efficiency of the British institutional provision towards those goals, and changes which occurred in teachers' thinking and classroom practices on their return, the study was to focus on the nature of the teachers' actual experiences during training. It was therefore set up as an open-ended exploratory investigation using ethnographic methods. My data consists of an extended series of recorded interviews with student-teachers and their tutors, classroom observation and audio-recording, and written assignments together with tutor feedback, all collected over the first year of their course.

What is a Good Reason?

Eight months into the course an incident occurred in the methodology class which seemed particularly telling. The tutor had asked the group to consider a number of activities for teaching vocabulary in the English classroom, and comment on their suitability in the Malaysian situation. One group had been presenting its thoughts to the whole class, when the spokesperson claimed that a certain activity would not be suitable since it did not allow integrated teaching of all four skills. At this point the tutor intervened. These are edited extracts from their exchange:

Tutor: Do you accept that everything you do in the class should be integrated – all four skills should be integrated?

N: We can't all four but it's better if we can get all four. I think it's better.

Tutor: Better from what point of view? Better for whom?

H: Better for the pupils *(unclear)* because *(unclear)* the new curriculum KBSR we are … we are encouraged to integrate all the four skills =

C: = in one lesson.

(General agreement)

....

C: The headmaster always *(unclear)* teach us to give the all the four skills.

....

Tutor: But simply because you were told something by someone on a course somewhere is *not* sufficient justification for doing it. I mean if this – you're probably right, maybe it's the best way to teach, but you need to know *why*. That is the best way to do it. You cannot just keep on saying 'but the head told me' or 'the course leader told me to', 'the government says' … 'because it's KBSR', it's not enough either. *Why* is it KBSR? I mean somebody dreamed it up: they had … what are their reasons for saying 'you must integrate'? It's not only integration, it's every issue. You *keep* doing that. You are just sliding out of responsibility for your own actions by saying 'That's the way it has to be, because that's the way it was last year and the year before' … That isn't enough. You need to think.

B: My my school you see (um) my headmistress take that stand because parents complain if we don't if children don't do written work in class.

(unclear interruption)

Tutor: OK so you're working your principle of teaching is 'I do what the parents want me to do' ....

(General subdued laughter)

In the rest of that lesson the divergence between the reasons offered by the student-teachers and those considered acceptable by the tutor was not reconciled. Some of the student participants reported the incident to me as memorable, and some were quite upset by the encounter.

This was by no means a typical exchange, but there was clearly some crucial negotiation going on here. Moreover the contradiction between their positions could be found running below the surface of the entire training programme, and it seemed to me to be central to what UK-based training is all about.

Training Critical Autonomous Individuals

There are a number of instances in my data which indicate that this moment was not an isolated incident but a particularly vivid example of a pervasive theme characterising the experience of the Malaysian teachers in their courses here. Interviews with course tutors, and tutors' comments on written assignments, demonstrate that one of their major aims was to develop critical and autonomous thinking, which they saw to be particularly lacking. They wanted to reduce students' dependence on tutors as sources of information and knowledge, and develop reliance on their own thinking and experience. They expected students to say why they believed what they thought, and to question what they read in the literature and heard from experts and others. A number of students also observed in interviews with me that they felt they were becoming more critical, analytical, autonomous, reflective, independent thinkers as a result of their courses here.

As articles by Brew, Hawkey, James and Watt (all in Greenall & Price, 1980) show, this is neither a new nor an unusual phenomenon. The implication of their various descriptions of the learning styles and attitudes to knowledge of certain overseas students, and how those differ from home tutors' expectations, is that courses in many different departments of British universities make the same kinds of demands on overseas students – to change their attitudes, behaviours and ways of thinking and develop an ability to be critical, independent thinkers. The question which arises, then, is how to explain this. What theoretical frameworks are there available which would illuminate the situation and explain why a movement towards critical and independent thinking is required?

Four Theoretical Frameworks

The exchange quoted above appears, then, to be a particularly clear example of an important and pervasive underlying issue in teaching across cultures, and a number of questions occur to me:

(a) Why did the tutor insist on principled reasons?

(b) Why did the students offer the particular reasons that they did?

(c) Why did the tutor not accept them as valid reasons?

(d) Why didn't the students catch on to what the tutor was wanting them to come up with (i.e. principles related to the professional practice of communicative language teaching)?

I will offer three possible theoretical frameworks which might inform answers to these questions. I will discuss some shortcomings of each of them before offering a fourth theoretical orientation which seems to me to be the most fruitful.

Cognitive Growth and Skills Learning

Viewed according to this theoretical orientation, overseas students are undergoing an ordinary educational process, which would be exactly the same as for home students going into higher education: they are learning how to think. No doubt there *is* something of this going on, but it seems inadequate as an explanation in this case since they are mature, experienced teachers, with at least three years of higher education already behind them. Furthermore, tutors in a variety of disciplines have contrasted South East Asian students and home students at the same stage of education as thinking differently (rather than less well). While a thinking skills approach might help to some extent to answer my questions above (particularly (d), perhaps), they seem to be less about undeveloped logic or inadequate cognitive rationality than a matter of understanding things in a different *way*. This leads us to consider the next possible explanatory framework.

Cross-Cultural Interface

A great deal of literature exists in the fields of inter-cultural communication and cross-cultural psychology which might inform our understanding of different teaching and learning styles and attitudes within the British and South Asian educational communities (for example, Asante & Gudykunst, 1989; Hofstede, 1982; Kim & Gudykunst, 1988). Hofstede has identified four key dimensions of cultural difference: Power Distance, Uncertainty Avoidance, Individualism vs.

Collectivism, and Masculinity vs. Femininity, which we might explore for their contribution to differences in ways of articulating educational discourse. Out of this cluster of cultural dimensions Jin & Cortazzi (1993) identified the interface between a collectivist Oriental culture and individualistic European culture as central to understanding the problems Chinese students have studying in Britain. Their solution is for both sides to make some degree of accommodation to the other *without losing their original cultural identity*, after a process of awareness raising about cultural differences.

This orientation seems to have a great deal to contribute to an understanding of all four of my questions. Belonging to a collectivist culture, Malaysians may be predisposed to thinking in terms of social cohesion, where it is important for schools, teachers and headmasters to comply with social norms rather than take individual principled stands. The tutor, on the other hand, as a member of an individualistic culture, may be predisposed to expect autonomy and personal responsibility in teachers' professional activities. If both parties were unaware of these different cultural dispositions then we might expect conflict to arise; and even if they were aware of them, the tutor might still see it as her professional responsibility not to accommodate.

However, this framework remains inadequate, I think, for two reasons. Firstly, it cannot take into account the asymmetric nature of the pedagogic relation, which means students' accounts never stand on equal terms with the tutor's. One side is *always* more powerful than the other: in this case, not only because of the tutor's status as a tutor, but because of the fact that she is standing in the shadow of colonial history, as well as being implicated in developed/underdeveloped country status relations. This means that social relations make it impossible for cross-cultural factors alone to fully explain what is happening in the interactions described in an earlier section.

Secondly, it is unhistoricised; it neglects consideration of historical processes of socio-cultural change, which are bound up with economic and technological change, dreams of progress, and the realities of global modernisation. As change occurs in the economic base of a society, its patterns of rural and urban dwelling, the sophistication of its infrastructure, modes of production, and types of employment, then different demands are made on the population. Different forms of literacy are required for example, different attitudes to work, different forms of knowledge, and different attitudes to knowledge and to learning. These changes occurred in Britain as we industrialised and entered modernity, and are occurring still as we move into late modernity (Giddens, 1991). Malaysia is now undergoing modernisation – moving from 'tradition' to 'modernity' – with an ambitious '2020' programme, which seeks to raise the country to developed nation status by that year. Some areas of the country are already considerably affected by the presence of multi-national companies. In this context our framework of analysis must make room for consideration of socio-cultural *change,* which the cross-cultural communication framework explicitly excludes.

Weber and Habermas, Rationalisation and Forms of Rationality

If, then, this classroom event is implicated in a historical process of change involving a transition, or possibly a clash, between *traditional* and *modern/late-modern* ways of thinking, learning and doing, we might usefully look to the social theory of Max Weber and Jurgen Habermas for guidance.

What Weber brings is the notion of historical change in culture, society and economy. In brief, he saw a connection between the process of economic change (industrialisation), and changes in ways of thinking, notably structures of rationality, as societies move from *tradition* to *modernity,* through a process of rationalisation. This transition involves the differentiation of cultural value spheres,[2] and of the forms of rationality associated with them. In particular he recognised the increasing use of *formal rationality* in modern capitalism, associated with law, calculation, any form of systemisation and teleological action, and its differentiation from *substantive* or *value rationality,* in which values such as equality, fraternity and caring are the basis for rational individual action (Albrow, 1990; Whimster & Lash, 1987). Following Weber, if Malaysia were following the same process of modernisation as Europe has, we would expect to find the same differentiation of value spheres and increased adoption of instrumental rationality. This process may be brought into particular focus in the sort of contact which takes place during overseas training, when the adoption of different patterns or modes of rationality might have to be accomplished very rapidly.

Weber offers a theory, but does not provide a tool for analysing the changes he describes. For this we may look to Habermas who, in his theory of social evolution, built on Weber's understanding of modernity and societal rationalisation in looking for a way through its contradictions[3] (Bernstein, 1985; Habermas, 1984; Thompson, 1984). Habermas introduces the concept of 'validity claims', which can be retrieved during the course of 'communicative action' in ideal speech situations, in the process of reconciling conflicts. We might, then, analyse the previously quoted exchange using the categories of validity claims that Habermas proposes (for reasons of space I am unable to provide a summary of his categories here, but see Thompson, 1984). What Habermas allows is a systematised way of identifying spheres of rationality by the appeals to validity claims (tacit or explicit) which are made in communication, and a criterion for assessing the interaction: the ideal of communicative rationality. In an ideal speech situation all validity claims would be reconcilable; the extent to which they are not reconciled is an effect of the differential power residing in participants. The first two categories, the cognitive-instrumental and the moral-practical, are the only ones which concern us here, if we assume that both sides of the interaction are being sincere and there is mutual comprehensibility.

In fact we can see that the possible reconciliation of conflicting validity claims which Habermas envisages in the pursuit of communicative rationality does not take place in the encounter illustrated above. This serves to demonstrate, or, conversely can be explained by, the fact that the classroom is *not* an ideal speech situation, but a pedagogical encounter between speakers, and discourses, of unequal status. There is an apparent tension here between two spheres of rationality. On the one hand we have the tutor's (implicit) requirement for reasons for teaching integrated skills according to *cognitive-instrumental reasoning,* using validity claims based on the 'truth' of principles of efficient language learning (Weber's 'formal rationality').[4] On the other hand we find the Malaysian teachers' use of *moral-practical reasoning,* using validity claims relating to the norms of the social networks in which they live and work, where reasoned arguments about instrumental goals may have to give way to the requirements of social cohesion (Weber's 'substantive' or 'value' rationality). The classroom interaction under consideration might therefore be seen as an example of an attempt to enact the modernisation process, at the level of individual thought processes, by the attempted discounting of moral-practical validity claims (considerations of respect for authority and social cohesion), and their replacement by instrumental ones (principles of effective teaching). Some teachers may resist this attempt more than others.

This framework seems to be productive for exploring the difficulties which some overseas students have, especially those from oriental and developing countries. Their struggle consists of making a transition away from an orientation towards text as authority, and knowledge as intimately bound within a matrix of socially defined values, distancing themselves from the authority of the text and the teacher, taking a critical stance towards both, separating themselves from everyday socially determined knowledge and treating themselves as autonomous producers of knowledge, demonstrating both the ability and the disposition to value truth and efficacy. This transition is required of them if they are to succeed in academic courses in the West, both in written work and classroom discussion.

All my questions are effectively addressed in this framework: the tutor insisted on principled reasons because they are required by the instrumental rationality prevailing in the culture in which she is immersed. Students offered reasons which reflected the values of their own culture, at a different stage of modernisation. The tutor did not accept them as valid because she was *being a teacher,* and students could not figure out what was acceptable because they were (as a group) still strongly immersed in values and ways of thinking relevant to their own educational system.

Yet I remain uneasy with this Weberian/Habermasian framework. Firstly it is not clear that the tutor *is* in fact pursuing a form of rationality associated with instrumental action – though she may well believe that she is. I maintain that she is requiring reasons that cannot in fact be objectively substantiated (in terms of truth, or efficacy of actions), given the current state of knowledge about second language acquisition, but that are simply a matter of what is appropriate in the educational world in which she herself operates. While it is claimed that justifications for pedagogic action can be grounded in a theoretical discourse, and should not appear to be simply those currently and temporarily accepted by the (professional) community, I believe that they are in fact more dependent on beliefs held within a particular professional culture than on objective knowledge. In this case, then, the origin of the tension lies not solely in either culturally or historically particular modes of reasoning, but also elsewhere.

Secondly, it seems unnecessarily rigid to adopt a framework which presupposes that a transition into instrumental rationality and cognitive-instrumental validity claims for arguments – at the expense of moral-practical validity claims – is a necessary part of the transition from tradition into modernity. Especially so since we are now in a late-modern age which gives indications that it may be moving away from many of the presuppositions Weber and Habermas have held about modernity – specifically those to do with objective knowledge and the separation of fact and value. Also it would be wrong to adopt a framework which did not allow alternatives, because some oriental societies show signs of evolving in ways that do not necessarily fit the Western model of social evolution, involving the dominance of instrumental rationality.

Nevertheless it seems worthwhile to take the essential insight from Habermas's conflicting validity claims argument, and extend it to a model which allows greater flexibility, which acknowledges that there is a dynamic to cultural evolution which makes cross-cultural educational interactions more than a simple matter of skills learning and knowledge transmission, yet does not presuppose that all societies will be following the Weberian pattern.

I propose then that we take the Habermasian model of different forms of rationality within differentiated cultural value spheres, with their associated validity claims, and extend it by making use of the Foucaultian concept of 'Orders of Discourse' (Fairclough, 1989: 28, 1992: 45). In this view, every order of discourse constitutes its own cultural sphere, and defines what validity claims are required to support arguments within that discourse: in other words, what will be counted as acceptable *reasons* in support of any position or proposition.

In short, every order of discourse has its own order of rationality, and negotiating one's way into a discourse involves using particular *grounds* of argumentation, as well as the conventional *forms* of argumentation, which are acceptable in that discourse.

Conclusion

Adopting a framework of orders of discourse allows us also to treat cross-cultural encounters as special cases of more general educational practices, making connections with work on academic literacies, and cultural reproduction and resistance. We can incorporate aspects of the notions of cultural difference and cross-cultural interaction, of historical socio-economic change, and associated changes in prevailing forms of rationality, without their limitations.

We can now see the classroom event which we started with in terms of a struggle between discourses. The Malaysian teachers were attempting to establish as legitimate their own discourse of traditional education, in which pedagogic practice can be justified by appeal to the authority of tradition, as inscribed in the curriculum, the headmaster, and the pressure which parents can put on schools if their own expectations are not met. The tutor was rejecting this discourse, and attempting to replace it with one in which the acceptable reasons for a course of action are ones which purport to derive from a personal position involving a commitment to principles of professional teaching practice. Since the tutor holds the power to grade assignments and examinations, and the student teachers' future careers depend on those grades, there is a strong incentive to adopt that discourse, at least in the short term. Nevertheless there is evidence of resistance, not least in the silence of many members of the group during this interaction.

Other classroom interactions in my data set offer examples of similar struggles. There is a struggle over resistance to or adoption of the current discourse of progressive education as it is taught on the Education component of the BEd programme, regarding for example the concept of reflective teaching, and the nature of children's knowledge and learning. The samples of written assignments I have available demonstrate other ongoing struggles over practices of argumentational justification and referencing which are required in written English academic discourse.

In my future data analysis I will be looking in my classroom and interview data for instances of discursive heterogeneity, or discourse mixing, which are the result of these struggles to reconcile competing and possibly incompatible discourses of education. These may be successful or unsuccessful, conscious or unconscious, and we may see some of them as instances of 'inter-discourse', similar to an inter-language, as steps along a progression towards a more fully evolved new discourse, combining existing elements which are culturally and historically specific.

Notes

1. This paper has benefited particularly from discussions with Dick Allwright, Roz Ivanic and members of the Lancaster Language Ideology and Power research group, whom I thank.
2. The religious, political, economic, aesthetic, erotic and intellectual.
3. Habermas finds problematic in the transition from clan to traditional to modern societies a progressive uncoupling of the life-world (where cultural tradition, social integration and personal identity are sustained and reproduced), from 'systems' (Thompson, 1984).
4. The tutor agreed in a subsequent interview that she would have accepted *any* reasons they came up with which they could relate to a principled understanding of the nature of teaching and learning.

References

Albrow, M. (1990) *Max Weber's Construction of Social Theory*. Basingstoke: Macmillan.
Asante, M. K. and Gudykunst, W. B. (eds) (1989) *Handbook of International and Intercultural Communication*. Newbury Park: Sage.
Bernstein, R. (ed.) (1985) *Habermas and Modernity*. Cambridge: Polity.
Fairclough, N. (1989) *Language and Power*. Harlow: Longman.
— (1992) *Discourse and Social Change*. Cambridge: Polity.
Giddens, A. (1991) *Modernity and Self-Identity: Self and society in the late modern age*. Cambridge: Polity.
Greenall, G. M. and Price, J. E. (eds) (1980) *Study Modes and Academic Development of Overseas Students*. London: British Council.
Habermas, J. (1984) *The Theory of Communicative Action Vol. 1 : Reason and the rationalisation of society*. London: Heinemann.
Hofstede, G. (1982) Dimensions of national cultures. In R. Rath, H. S. Asthana, D. Sinha, and J. B. P. Sinha (eds) *Diversity and Unity in Cross-Cultural Psychology*. Lisse: Swets and Zeitlinger.
Jin, L. and Cortazzi, M. (1993) Cultural orientation and academic language use. In D. Graddol, L. Thompson, and M. Byram (eds) *Language and Culture* (pp. 84–97). Clevedon: BAAL and Multilingual Matters.
Kim, Y. Y. and Gudykunst, W. B. (eds) (1988) *Theories in Intercultural Communication*. Newbury Park: Sage.
Thompson, J. (1984) *Studies in the Theory of Ideology*. Cambridge: Polity.
Whimster, S. and Lash, S. (eds) (1987) *Max Weber, Rationality and Modernity*. London: Allen and Unwin.

8 Phraseological Competence and Written Proficiency

A. P. COWIE and PETER HOWARTH
University of Leeds

Introduction

Following a steady expansion of scholarly activity over the past 20 years in Eastern as well as Western Europe, phraseology has now come into its own as a major focus of pure and applied research. Its coming of age is reflected in a number of major projects and marked by several recent international conferences.[1] Interestingly, the study of phraseology in an applied linguistics context precedes by some decades these recent large-scale developments and can be traced back to the work of H. E. Palmer and A. S. Hornby in Japan in the 1930s, and to Palmer's perceptive recognition that memorized stable word-combinations represent a formidable obstacle to successful language learning. Palmer and Hornby pioneered phraseological research – Palmer's *Second Interim Report on English Collocations* of 1933, on which Hornby collaborated, is a neglected classic, stressing as it does the arbitrary, non-rule-governed nature of word-combinations, and the fact that they have to be learned as wholes. Thus they can claim credit for being the first to use 'collocation' in something like its present-day sense, incidentally pre-dating J. R. Firth's use of the term by 18 years (Firth, 1951).

For those interested in second language acquisition the great value of a phraseological perspective is the light it can throw on aspects of language production and the mechanisms underlying learners' developing competence. This paper is concerned with writing, specifically student academic writing in the humanities and social sciences, and focuses on the contribution made by phraseological knowledge at various levels of proficiency to the work of native and non-native writers.

80

The body of material examined for our paper is small and forms part of an ongoing joint investigation of student writing. This larger project is in turn an extension of Howarth's doctoral research (Howarth, in press). We focus here on two sets (one native, one non-native) of four essays each, all of between 1500 and 3000 words and all dealing with topics in applied linguistics. Howarth's recent research, and Cowie's earlier analyses of phraseology in the quality press (Cowie, 1991, 1992), showed that so-called 'restricted collocations' – *gain access, concede defeat, adopt a policy,* and so on – made up a consistently high proportion of all combinations of a given structural type in texts in which authorial detachment and neutrality were at a premium. As can be seen from the examples, this major category consists of word-combinations in which one element (here the verb) has a specialized meaning determined by the other element (here the noun). Restricted collocations can be broken down into a number of sub-types, along a scale or continuum, taking account of the relative variability of individual collocations (Cowie, 1981, 1986, 1994; Howarth, 1994, in press). Such sub-categorization seems likely to provide reliable criteria by which the performance of able writers can be assessed, and the deficiencies of the less able pinpointed, and it was with a view to testing these assumptions that we embarked on our follow-up project.

Theoretical Assumptions

Our analytical approach, which can be traced back to the work of Russian phraseologists of the 1960s and earlier (for accounts in English of this work, see Weinreich, 1969; Arnold, 1986; Cowie, 1978), focuses on collocations and idioms as combinations of abstract elements, not on their possible realizations in texts. The arbitrary dependencies we study in phraseology involve lexemes or roots, not their morpho-syntactic exponents (Mitchell, 1971). The following example may help to make clear the distinction we are drawing:

COLLOCATION	Realizations in text
'implement' + 'method'	*implement* the *method*
	the direct *method* not ... *difficult to implement*

The sequences *implement* the *method* and *the direct method* not ... *difficult to implement* both crop up in the same text by a native writer. However, they can be regarded as two out of several possible realizations of the one collocation 'implement' (verb root) + 'method' (noun root).

There are several advantages to be gained by adopting this perspective. The first is that the analyst has a principled basis for regarding as a collocation two or more items in a text that may be relatively remote, and at first sight unrelated.

Consider the following example:

> ... *dependent more on the <u>conditions</u> which <u>prevail</u> outside*
>
> *the classroom than those <u>created</u> within ...*

COLLOCATIONS: 'conditions' + 'prevail'; 'create' + 'conditions'

There are actually two verb-noun collocations here: the noun + verb collocation 'conditions' + 'prevail' – whose exponents happen to be quite close – but also the verb + noun collocation 'create' + 'conditions' – whose realizations are separated by seven word-forms. Notice, by the way, that the difference between singular *condition* and plural *conditions* may be semantically significant, as here, where *conditions* means 'circumstances' and collocability is affected. (We say *conditions prevail*, not **a condition prevails*. Cf. *a condition is/conditions are imposed.*)

A further justification for the approach is that collocational restriction – like co-occurrence restriction – operates at the lexemic level. The narrow choice of verb represented by 'prevail' in relation to 'conditions', say, is precisely the same whether we are actually faced by *the conditions which prevail, conditions that had prevailed* or *conditions prevailing*. If we wish to define and classify collocations in terms of the dependence of one element on another, we must deal with them in abstraction from the forms they assume in given utterances.

Collocations are often described as fixed and recurrent word-combinations (Benson *et al.*, 1986: ix; cf. Summers *et al.,* 1995: xi, xvi). But both parts of this description are misleading. Typically, collocations are not fixed but variable to a limited and arbitrary degree. As for frequency, it can be shown that individual restricted collocations may recur to only a limited extent within a given text or across several texts devoted to the same topic. It is best to think of a collocation as a familiar (or institutionalized), stored (or memorized) word-combination with limited and arbitrary variation. If we include among these criteria the optional criterion of semantic opaqueness, we have defined idioms as well as collocations. The various criteria are set out at (1):

(1) Characteristics of collocations and idioms

+	familiar	(institutionalized)
+	stored	(memorized)
+	limited and arbitrary variability	(restricted)
+/–	semantically opaque	(unmotivated)

Putting idioms on one side for a moment, and starting from the idea of internal variability or restriction, we can recognize four possibilities, yielding four sub-types of collocation:

(2) Sub-types of collocation

(a) INVARIABLE COLLOCATION

break a journey

foot the bill

(b) COLLOCATION WITH LIMITED CHOICE AT ONE POINT

take/have/be given precedence (over NP)

give/allow/permit access to NP

have/feel/experience a need (for NP)

(c) COLLOCATION WITH LIMITED CHOICE AT TWO POINTS

find/experience trouble/difficulty in DOING NP

get/have/receive a lesson/tuition/instruction (in NP)

(d) OVERLAPPING COLLOCATIONS

convey a point

communicate a view

*communicate regrets

*get across condolences

The first, type (a), clearly, is where there is no variation at all. (Consider *break a journey, foot the bill.*) However, this type does not occur in our texts, and for purposes of the present investigation can be ignored. A further type, (b), allows some variation at one point, as in *take/have/be given precedence (over NP)*. Yet another category, type (c), is one in which limited choice is possible at two points in the collocation – consider *find/experience trouble/difficulty in DOING NP*.

A further category, type (d), is the most problematical, and the most interesting, since it combines apparent openness with actual restriction. (A perfectly open collocation would be one which – like *open the window* or *shut the door* –

was formed by general principles of co-occurrence.) Collocations of type (d) are further illustrated by the examples at (3) (consider *convey a point* in the left-hand panel). Of course, other verbs synonymous with *convey* can also combine with *point: express, communicate, get across,* and if we keep that verb selection constant, we can substitute *argument, view, opinion* and *message* for *point.* Here there is complete intercollocability of verbs and nouns, and we have a so-called 'cluster' of overlapping collocations:

(3) Overlapping collocations

CLUSTER A		CLUSTER B	
convey	point	convey	regrets
express	argument	express	condolences
communicate	view	*communicate	
get across	opinion	*get across	
	message		

But consider a related cluster, cluster B (in the right-hand panel). Here we have, in much the same sense as before ('pass (a message) from one person to another'), the verbs *convey* and *express,* though now in collocation with *regrets* and *condolences.* We notice, however, that *communicate* and *get across* are questionable, or even unacceptable, collocates (see Cowie, 1986). Here the overlap is partial and certain plausible combinations are arbitrarily blocked.

The notion of cluster is of crucial importance. If *convey* in fact means the same in both clusters, where the verbs are synonymous, then the fact that *communicate* and *get across* do not operate in Cluster B is idiosyncratic, and within the domain of phraseology. It is also a troublesome detail which foreign learners – and even native speakers – cannot be depended on to know. A possible result might be the transfer of collocates from one cluster to one or more neighbouring clusters (viz. **communicate condolences*). In fact Howarth's work has shown that less proficient learners often fall into the traps laid by overlapping clusters (Howarth, in press). On the other hand, the successful use of clusters could be a mark of proficiency among native writers. This was to be one of the hypotheses we tested as we examined the work of these writers.

Findings

The native-speaker data consisted of four essays by third-year undergraduates – all set and marked for content and language a year before this analysis was embarked on. The essays were all concerned with language teaching theory, and were chosen as representative of performance at first class, upper IIi, lower IIi and lower IIii levels. The analysis points to one reasonably firm, quantitative conclusion that applies generally, and a number of more tentative, but none the less suggestive, conclusions that apply in individual cases.

The general point is that the percentage of restricted collocations (taking (b), (c) and (d) together) found in an essay, compared with the percentage of combinations of the same syntactic type which are not restricted in any way, is a reliable measure of the written proficiency of its author. This conclusion closely matches the one that Howarth arrived at earlier (in press) from his study of a much larger body of data. It holds true in the present study whether one considers collocations at the abstract level or their various morpho-syntactic realizations. In the following table we set out for each of the four native writers – going from most to least proficient – the proportion of restricted collocations (as a percentage of all combinations of the same verb + object pattern). We also indicate for each writer the corresponding percentage of realizations.

(4) Quantitative measures

Text	Essay mark (%)	Realizations (%)	Collocations (%)
A	72	36.95	32.50
B	68	31.03	31.58
C	62	28.87	28.13
D	54	18.87	17.31

The second set of figures matches the different proficiency levels less closely. Table 5, which shows the numbers of type (d) collocations used by each student in comparison with all collocations and idioms, indicates that A, B, and C – the most proficient writers – all use a relatively high number.

(5) Relation of type (d) collocations to other types

Text	Realizations		Collocations	
	(d)	(b) + (c)	(d)	(b) + (c)
A	19	34	12	26
B	15	27	13	24
C	13	28	13	27
D	2	10	2	9

At the same time, there is very little difference between the actual proportions of type (d) used by those students – about half in each case. However, there are considerable differences in the way these collocations are used. Consider writer A. What is striking about A is that although she uses 12 distinct (d) collocations, five are variants from two clusters. The combinations *implement the method, apply the method* come from one cluster, and *fulfil a requirement, fulfil a condition, meet a condition* come from another. Student A rings the changes on the fairly limited resources she deploys, but she does so with precision. Notice, though, that one must know the acceptable linkages in a cluster – such as the one below – and be sure to avoid the non-linkages.

(6) Overlapping collocations in a student essay

Cluster C	
meet	condition
fulfil	term
satisfy	requirement
comply with	
conform to	

Student B is also highly competent, but in comparison with A, B depends more on knowledge of distinct collocations than on skill in making varied use of the same clusters. B also repeats collocations less often than A. (The relationship between realization percentage and collocation percentage for A is 36.95% to 32.50%; the corresponding relationship for B is 31.03% to 31.58%.)

Student C's chief weakness seems to be his liking for innovative collocations in a context which calls for conventional ones. Generally, he is a competent user of restricted collocations and successful in producing variants. However, he sometimes strikes a false note stylistically through his fondness for creative combinations (*fuel a lesson, regiment a course*) and by some imprecision in his use of well-established collocations (*instil a logical approach, inhibit an application*).

The least proficient student, D, uses half the percentage of restricted collocations of A and B, while of those he selects, the majority (8 out of 10) are of the least flexible types – those which make fewest demands on memory. His errors are often a matter of co-occurrence (i.e. semantic) restriction rather than collocational restriction – consider his choice of *expanding* (rather than *extending* or *developing*) *the communication abilities.* This example suggests that D is still grappling with broad semantic distinctions rather than managing collocational niceties. (The verb *expand* requires an object whose referent is perceived as a volume or space: thus *expand one's vocabulary* or knowledge, but *extend one's abilities*.)

Non-Native Student Writing

Moving on now to examine learner language from this same perspective, it is clearly of great significance to second language learners and their teachers that native-speaker language production is characterized by the appropriate use of prefabricated, memorized lexical complexes and is not purely the product of spontaneous generative processes. The assumption underlying this study is that teachers' judgements of learners' academic performance will be affected in some way by its phraseological features. At present, however, little is known in detail about phraseological competence in a second language, nor about how it is acquired. The examination of learner performance discussed here can be understood as a search for evidence of such competence and it is hoped thereby to relate learners' phraseological performance to some other measure of second language proficiency, an intuitively plausible correlation.

The evidence can be categorized in the following ways:

(1) quantitative: % of restricted vs open collocations

(2) stylistic: effects of competence or lack of competence

(3) psycholinguistic: learners' strategies underlying phraseological performance.

There are particular problems in analysing learner language within the framework outlined above. Firstly, in the identification and categorisation of word combinations produced in a second language, the number of grammatical errors makes the automatic analysis of L2 writing even more difficult than L1 writing. The analyst must be actively engaged in interpretation from the outset in order to uncover the collocational lexemes underlying the surface forms, and there is a need at times to reconstruct the probable target collocation. The second problem peculiar to academic writing is one of attribution. There is a recurring doubt about the authenticity of some combinations encountered: the influence of what has been read and assimilated into a student's text may prevent some collocations from being safely regarded as evidence of the writer's own competence. There may also be unacknowledged direct quotation. Similar doubts could, however, be raised over native student writing.

In spite of these difficulties, the method has been fairly rigorously tested as a means of comparing the performance of native and advanced non-native writers of academic English in a large-scale study of about 200,000 words of text (Howarth, in press). The non-native part of the present study examines four essays written by overseas MA students of applied linguistics from four countries in Africa, Asia and Europe, who are themselves teachers of English. In the description of the data, attention will be drawn to certain features of their writing that suggest fruitful directions for further study.

Quantitative Measures

If it is true that mature native writer performance is characterized by the use of an appropriate proportion of conventional phraseology, is a lower level of linguistic proficiency reflected in a lower phraseological density? Attempts to discover a correlation either with scores on a language proficiency test (the Leeds University EAP test) or with the academic grades awarded to the pieces of writing have failed to reveal a clear direct relationship: neither measure sufficiently discriminates among a group of supposedly advanced learners. The four texts are presented here in order of academic grade:

(7) **Comparison between percentages of restricted collocations (and their realizations) and other measures of proficiency**

Text	Essay mark (%)	Test score (%)	Realizations (%)	Collocations (%)
I	65	75	21.8	18.75
II	61	97	27.3	28.3
III	55	80	12.8	11.1
IV	55	83	23.3	18.75

In terms of rank order, there appears to be no correlation between any two columns, suggesting that further work needs to be done to understand phraseological competence in relation to a quantitative measure of linguistic proficiency. However, comparison between the NNS texts as a whole and the four NS writers in their percentage use of restricted collocations produces rather satisfying evidence of an overlap in proficiency. As lecturers might expect, the more proficient non-native can outperform the weaker native, at least by this criterion:

(8) **Comparison between the collocational densities of NS and NNS written texts**

%	37	31	29	27	23	22	19	13
NS	A	B	C				D	
NNS				II	IV	I		III

However, this is clearly too simplistic to be taken at face value. While the NS phraseological figures do correlate with general proficiency, the NNS figures do not. In the absence of a valid concurrent measurement, it can be claimed that Text II was written by the student with the most expert grasp of appropriate academic style (27% approaches the figures produced by the more proficient native writers), giving the impression of a confident mastery of the material, while Text III (13% stands out as a significantly low figure) gives the impression of hesitancy and less familiarity with the conventional modes of academic expression. The other two texts, however, do not fit neatly into this pattern: Text IV would not be regarded as a proficient piece of writing, yet the phraseological density is quite high (23%), while the much better written essay, Text I, scores slightly lower phraseologically (22% of realizations).

A possible explanation for this lack of correlation is that, while native writers can be assumed to be reasonably homogeneous in their linguistic development (even though some will have advanced further than others at any particular academic level), non-native students come to universities in this country with a very wide range of experience, attitudes, aptitude and strategies, resulting in very variable levels of proficiency in individual components of linguistic competence. Further evidence may confirm that this measure (of collocational density) represents a necessary but not sufficient condition for competence: it may prove possible to establish a rough minimum level below which a writer is unlikely to perform proficiently.

Additionally, the non-native data confirms that it is not the idiomatic end of the phraseological spectrum that requires attention. Firstly, idioms are relatively few in number (3–4% of all collocation types). Secondly, they are controlled accurately and appropriately: for example, *call sth into question, keep sth in view, take place.* In contrast to the difficulties encountered in the appropriate use of restricted collocations, it is clear that idioms are unproblematic.

As was found in the NS data, of all restricted collocations the majority are found towards the free end of the range. However, in contrast to NS writers, NNS writers use a much greater proportion of collocations that are quite open and present no phraseological challenge. It may be that these learners are deliberately avoiding an area of language use they know to be problematic.

Stylistic Effects of Competence

The phraseologically competent writer is, among other things, able to maintain appropriate collocational relationships even when the two or more parts are separated in the text:

> *intelligence <u>tests</u> are not language free but are <u>conducted</u> through the medium of language*

It is clearly easy for these connections to be broken, perhaps when a writer is less aware of phraseological constraints and feels under pressure from other linguistic demands during composition:

> *?<u>Needs analysis</u> as a technique used to specify the learners' needs is <u>brought</u> <u>about</u> by focusing ...*

Another feature of mature writing is the linking of collocations into larger sequences, which can produce a highly admired effect of fluency and confidence. The present data does not provide much direct evidence of such skills:

> *the <u>techniques</u> good language learners <u>adopt</u> to <u>learn</u> a <u>language</u>*

One example stands out clearly:

> *... <u>effort</u> has been <u>made</u> to <u>meet</u> the <u>needs</u> and <u>preferences</u> of an individual learner which have always existed but only recently have started to be <u>taken</u> <u>into</u> <u>account</u>. In the effort to <u>meet</u> <u>them</u>, it is assumed that the <u>learner</u> has been <u>given</u> some <u>responsibility</u> for his/her own learning.*

This was written without quotation marks by the most proficient writer in the group, though the explanation for such phraseological expertise was provided by a reference in brackets, which turns out to be the source of most of this extract. However, this should not be dismissed as mere lifting; a close analysis shows that attempts have successfully been made to adapt and assimilate the original (presented here as plain text, with the student's contributions in bold):

> *... <u>effort</u> has been <u>made</u> to <u>meet</u> the <u>needs</u> and <u>preferences</u> of an individual learner **which have always existed but only recently have started to be <u>taken</u> <u>into</u> <u>account</u>**. In the effort to <u>meet</u> **<u>them</u>**, it is assumed that **the <u>learner</u>** has been <u>given</u> some <u>responsibility</u> for his/**her** own learning.*

Evidence of this kind provides an insight into the production process and possible evidence of mechanisms underlying acquisition. It would seem that the writer has a high level of awareness of phraseology and makes a conscious effort to forge appropriate collocational links. An additional point of interest in this extract is that it illustrates the problem of co-ordinated collocations and of attribution of learner writing. While *meet the needs* is a conventional combination, *?meet the preferences* appears less standard. This might have been an example of learner mis-collocation, but in fact is taken from the native original.

Learners' Strategies

The lack of native-like phraseological performance in certain advanced uses of a language by a non-native writer can have unintended effects on clarity and intelligibility (Howarth, 1994). It is the category nearer the free end of the spectrum where errors are made and where phraseological deviance can result in the breakdown of sense. The problem for the learner lies in distinguishing between what is an entirely free combination and one that is in an arbitrary way restricted. With limited phraseological resources, learners may seek ways to maximize the effectiveness of what they have. Two possible strategies can be identified:

(1) Extension by analogy

In cases where a single writer makes repeated use of a verb in combination with a range of nouns, it is conceivable that he or she has memorized a core collocation which is either restricted or technical and uses it as the basis for the production of other collocations. Thus, it could be claimed that a learner internalizes *acquire a language* and, appropriately, produces *acquire proficiency*. The same explanation is suggested for *adopt techniques (←adopt methods?)*. However, this mechanism will not always prove successful (each pair of examples occurred in a single text):

> *?adopt ways (←adopt an approach?)*

> *?carry out principles (←carry out research?)*

This approach to acquisition differs from the development of overlapping clusters that native speakers achieve, of which there is little evidence in these essays.

(2) Experimentation

It seems plausible that learners (more than native speakers) become conscious of the semantic distinctiveness of the type of restricted collocations characteristic of formal writing. The large number of verbs used with specialized meanings, such as *adopt, draw, follow, pay, perform,* may encourage them to believe that the combining of figurative senses of verbs with abstract nouns is a fully creative productive mechanism. Although *?trigger the focus* and *?ignite the emergence* may be quite easily intelligible, and in certain registers their use might be applauded as evidence of positive risk taking, in a controlled and neutral style they seem to produce an undesirable lack of precision.

Conclusion

To sum up, it has been shown, firstly, that phraseology is a significant component of native and non-native proficiency. The tendency to resort to memorized routines operates more generally than simply in those styles produced under the pressure of time (such as journalistic prose). One useful property of such non-innovative standard collocations in academic prose is that they do not draw attention to themselves. Their use is designed to produce a neutral, unobtrusive style that is best suited to the objective presentation of facts.

Secondly, these studies have suggested that writers' knowledge of individual collocations does not seem to develop through repeated use or through massive exposure to them in the writings of others. Familiarization with collocations may come about through a gradually growing perception of their idiosyncratic properties and specifically of the arbitrariness with which their components select each other. It is these more abstract phraseological properties that learners must acquire knowledge of rather than simply being exposed to large numbers of individual combinations.

Finally, we hope to have shown that valuable insights are yielded by quite small quantities of data. An interest in language acquisition requires a focus on the individual language user, and, while it is true that many more individuals need to be studied, a simple quantitative approach that draws gross averages from the collective performance of a large number of writers will not reveal what those writers are doing nor how their competence is being developed.

We recognize that what we have presented goes only a small way towards an understanding of the acquisition of phraseology. However, the descriptive methodology is proving its worth and, it is hoped, will provide a firm basis for future exploration.

Notes

1. Recent major conferences include Europhras 88 (devoted to contrastive phraseology) held at Strasbourg in 1988, the Séminaire International sur la Phraséologie, held in Hull, Canada in 1993 and the International Symposium on Phraseology organized at Leeds in 1994.

References

Arnold, I. V. (1986) *The English Word.* Third edition. Moscow: Vysšaja Škola.
Benson, M., Benson, R. and Ilson, R. (1986) *The BBI Combinatory Dictionary of English.* Amsterdam: John Benjamins.
Cowie, A. P. (1978) The place of illustrative material and collocations in the design of a learner's dictionary. In P. Strevens (ed.) *In Honour of A. S. Hornby.* Oxford: Oxford University Press.
— (1981) The treatment of collocations and idioms in learners' dictionaries. *Applied Linguistics* 2.3, 223–35.
— (1986) Collocational dictionaries – a comparative view. In M. Murphy (ed.) *Proceedings of the Fourth Anglo-Soviet English Studies Seminar.* London: British Council.
— (1991) Multiword units in newspaper language. In S. Granger (ed.) *Perspectives on the English Lexicon.* Louvain-la-Neuve: Cahiers de l'Institut de Linguistique de Louvain.

— (1992) Multi-word units and communicative language teaching. In P. Arnaud and H. Béjoint (eds) *Vocabulary and Applied Linguistics*. London: Macmillan.

— (1994) Phraseological dictionaries – some East–West comparisons. Paper presented at the International Symposium on Phraseology, University of Leeds.

Firth, J. R. (1951) Modes of meaning. *Essays and Studies* 4 (Reprinted in Firth (1957) *Papers in Linguistics* 1934–1951).

Howarth, P. (1994) The phraseology of learners' academic writing. Paper presented at the International Symposium on Phraseology, University of Leeds.

— (in press) *A Computer-Assisted Study of Collocations in Academic Prose*. Tübingen: Niemeyer.

Mitchell, T. F. (1971) Linguistic 'goings-on': Collocations and other lexical matters arising on the syntagmatic record. *Archivum Linguisticum* NS 2, 25–69.

Palmer, H. E. (1933) *Second Interim Report on English Collocations*. Tokyo: Institute for Research in English Teaching.

Summers, D. *et al.* (1995) *The Longman Dictionary of Contemporary English*. 3rd edn. London: Longman.

Weinreich, U. (1969) Problems in the analysis of idioms. In J. Puhvel (ed.) *Substance and Structure of Language*. Berkeley and Los Angeles: University of California Press.

9 The Occurrence of 'Occurance' (and 'Alot' of Other Things 'Aswell'): Patterns of errors in undergraduate English

ALISON WRAY
University of Wales Swansea

Introduction

Across all disciplines, decisions, individual, departmental or institution-wide, have to be made about how to deal with non-standard English in academic writing. To what extent is it part of the university teacher's job to correct in detail an essay which has, say, verbless 'sentences', freestanding subordinate clauses, non-standard punctuation or spelling, or awkward structure? Is it sufficient to pepper the margin with wry comments about spell-check software and proof-reading? Some would argue that they have better things to do than make up for what they see as the deficits of primary and secondary education, and that students with poor writing skills should be directed to a dedicated writing-support unit in the institution.

On the other hand, there are pragmatic arguments for responding proactively to errors in the written English of our students. One is that writing-support units do not have the resources to deal with the numbers who could benefit from help: in our survey 72% of students made one or more errors with the apostrophe and 87.5% made spelling errors. These, and many of the other error types we have logged, may well be considered superficial problems in comparison to a characterisation of 'sub-literacy', but it is undoubtedly the case that many employers

94

judge graduates harshly if there are non-standard features in letters of application (Jeffs, 1985: 2f). Perhaps most vulnerable to such judgements by the outside world are students of English and Linguistics, because public perception associates the study of these subjects with being 'good at English'. Austin-Ward (1986) reports the four most common reasons for college students wanting further English tuition as being to: 'learn to spell', 'learn correct grammar', 'learn to "speak properly"'and 'choose and use correct words' (p. 37).

Whilst some take the view that competence in basic writing skills should be a prerequisite for entry into tertiary education, others would argue that many of the 'standards' we expect are no longer applicable to most types of written English; the language of advertising and journalism, to give one example, demonstrates that the 'sentence' adheres to its grammar-book definition in ever fewer communicational contexts. This makes academic writing an even narrower and more specialised variety than we tend to think, and one which students cannot be expected to know when they arrive. Nevertheless, the reasoning continues, the skills required for this variety are not intrinsically mysterious, and students will learn expressive rigour, the finer points of 'standard' English and the discipline to adhere to them consistently, if we give them the chance.

Another argument that resonates greatly in the outside world is that anything students with Qualified Teacher Status (QTS) leave university still doing will get ploughed straight back into the education of the next generation. David Pascall, Chairman of the National Curriculum Council, reportedly said in 1993 that 'thousands of teaching staff need to correct their own grammar, punctuation and spoken English if they [are] to act as proper role models for children' (*Daily Mail,* 16.4.93).

We may, of course, question whether things are actually any worse now than they were before. A report of an essay competition run for sixth formers by the *Daily Telegraph* in 1985 observed that 'the spelling ... was often incredibly bad, even in some of the most intelligent essays' (*Daily Telegraph,* 9.12.85, quoted in Jeffs, 1985: 1).

The Bullock Report provides evidence of concerns about teachers' written English in the mid-seventies:

> Essays by college of education students ... contained numerous errors of spelling, punctuation, and construction, and were a disturbing indication that the students who wrote them were ill-equipped to cope with the language demands they would meet in schools. Observations to the same effect have been made to us by heads, who have complained of the poor standard of written expression of some of the young teachers who have joined their schools. (DES, 1975: 4)

Furthermore, as the same document points out (p. 3), the Newbolt Report of 1921 was also logging a dissatisfaction on the part of employers with the quality of written English in their young recruits.

Today we read of a 'real slide' (*Observer*, 24.7.94) in traditional skills that have rendered literacy levels amongst school leavers 'a national disgrace' with 48% of 16–18 year olds 'poor at written English' (Queen's English Society, reported in *THES*, 17.6.94). Blame is levelled largely at preferred primary and secondary teaching methods over the last three decades, which found 'little value in grammatical correctness' (Marenbon, 1994: 16). Our serving, then, is the tasty tertiary topping on a large and well-baked political hot potato.

Marenbon views the Bullock Report of 1975 as having encouraged the perpetuation of a laxity in standards, and quotes a recommendation that 'in correcting work, teachers should not pay too much attention to "surface features" (such as spelling and grammar)' (Marenbon, 1994: 17).

However, the approach was rather more subtle than this suggests. Whilst it is indeed stated in the report that 'repeated failure reinforces a poor self-image, and the correction of work can make matters worse unless its purposes are carefully worked out' (DES, 1975: 167), constructive suggestions are then made for achieving greater accuracy, such as talking the individual pupil through the errors (see, for example, the approach taken by Jeffs, 1985).

School and university teachers alike may yearn for the resourcing necessary to offer such individual tutorials on the finer points of expression and presentation. Yet at tertiary level, certainly, the increase in student numbers has placed greater strain on staff time, as well as creating a greater need: we now have in the system students whose written English would previously have been symptomatic of their exclusion. Indeed we do not need to invoke a general fall in standards to explain the changes observed in undergraduate writing – just the broadening of the university intake.

The arguments for a prescriptive view of students' errors in written English can be summarised as follows:

• Those who do not have access to an adequate range of varieties of written English are at a disadvantage in the employment market. The variety of educated written English which we expect from graduates is one which they should learn if they want to belong to that elite class.

• If trainee teachers do not learn the variety associated with educated writing, they will be unable to teach it. The stronger line taken by the requirements of the National Curriculum for English makes this a serious concern.

For linguists, both the defence of standards they have achieved themselves and the protection of students in a cruel, judgemental world conflict with a general preference for a descriptive approach to language. Even if individuals can find ways of reconciling descriptivism and prescriptivism in their own minds, it is far from clear that the subtleties of the argument are received without confusion by the student.

A descriptive approach to data such as that gathered in our study opens up numerous questions of interest that help us monitor contemporary change:

- 18-year-olds are writing *alot, aswell, infact* while their older (mature student) classmates look on in bewilderment. Why *alot* and not, apparently, *abit* or *afew*? Why now?[1] Is the apparent speed of this development real, or is it an illusion attributable to the broadened intake?

- Are teachers simply ambivalent about certain errors, or are they being taught as correct? If teachers are under-confident in their own command of grammar, spelling and punctuation, how does that affect the way they teach and correct work?

- Which of these 'errors' will be standard for future generations, and which will turn out to have been just temporary blips?

- What role might corpora projects like COBUILD play in legitimising forms currently considered non-standard?

- How much longer can the apostrophe survive?

- Is written English being re-formed in the context of a new oral culture, where children don't write letters any more and an e-mail message looks odd if it is written in a formal style?

It is in the light of this uneasy balance between prescriptivism and descriptivism that the following findings are reported. Even the most prescriptive may find some 'errors' they could tolerate, for we all have our price. Other transgressions might offend even the most descriptive, such as the mis-spelling of proper names, or inconsistency within the work of one individual: both could be seen as more symptomatic of carelessness than legitimate radicalism. It is recognised, then, that each reader will react differently to aspects of our selection and may feel that some examples are questionable as illustrations of an 'error'.

Types of 'Error' in Undergraduate English

The research at the University College of Ripon and York St John (UCRYSJ) aims to look for patterns in 'errors' and identify which are most common. The long-term aims of the project are to (a) monitor differences in the profiles of successive incoming cohorts, (b) monitor the development of skills during degree programmes by comparing entry and exit profiles, (c) compare significant subgroups of students, such as school leavers and mature students, (d) broaden the study to other institutions for comparison and, where possible, to pool results.

The results presented here are drawn from the pilot study conducted in 1995. The corpus totals *c.*173,000 words, being the first linguistics essay (1,500–2,000 words) submitted by 104 first year undergraduates on Language Studies programmes. Although some word-processed essays will have undergone a computer spell- or grammar-check, there are good reasons for not regarding this as detrimental to the study:

- It is evident from our data that these checks are not always used on word-processed essays;
- Any distortion created by the use of such software only strengthens the validity of our remaining observations;
- Computer software is just one of several tools (dictionaries, getting a friend to read an essay through) that students are free to apply before submission;
- We are not particularly interested in knowing which words a student cannot spell from memory, how s/he first constructs a sentence, or how the punctuation looks before checking. There are, after all, few people who *never* need to check a spelling or rewrite an awkward passage. Rather, we are interested in the finished result, because this reflects (a) the commitment to accuracy, (b) the care taken to assure quality, and (c) the ability to spot potential errors.

In contrast, exam scripts would provide only limited insight into the actual awareness of the writer, for exam conditions are not conducive to wordsmithing.

As electronic scanning is not practical for handwritten data, error types were highlighted in the scripts by hand using a colour code (thus categorisations could be double-checked at any time). The examples were then logged in a database. Besides spelling, the apostrophe, and word-breaks (reported below) a number of other categories have been logged for analysis, including: sentence construction, punctuation, lexical choice, agreement/pronoun cohesion, style and awkward structure.

Results of Preliminary Analysis: Apostrophes, spelling & word-breaks

Apostrophe

— 72% of students made one or more errors in the use of the apostrophe;
— 51% of students made more than one error per 1000 words;
— of the total sample (not just the error-making group):

— 29% put an apostrophe in possessive *its*;
— 21% used an apostrophe in non-possessive plurals;
— 26% omitted the apostrophe in possessive plurals;
— 39% omitted the apostrophe in possessive singulars.

A reasonable hypothesis to test would be that some students simply omit the apostrophe in all circumstances (except perhaps to put it in possessive *its*). However, an examination of the distribution of errors indicates that whilst 50/104 (48%) omitted at least one apostrophe, only 13 (12.5%) omitted *both* singular *and* plural apostrophes; 24 (23%) omitted *only singular* apostrophes; 13 (12.5%) omitted *only plural* apostrophes. Some students undoubtedly avoid possessive plurals entirely (and so never get them wrong).

Spelling

87.5% of students made one or more spelling error. Furthermore, many students seem to be painfully aware of their inability to spell words 'instinctively'. In informal discussions unrelated to the research, three students agreed that their strategy for coping with an impending spelling problem was to go back and re-write the whole sentence to avoid the word.

Classification

For the purposes of this study, a detailed classificatory system for the spelling errors was required – more detailed than, for example, that of the Scottish Council for Research in Education (1961: 172ff) or Upward (1992: 86f). Diagnostic approaches focused on primary children (e.g. Peters, 1979: 17f; Read, 1986) were also clearly inappropriate. The following schema was devised for the pilot study:

— substitutions:
    — s for c and c for s (e.g. absense, practise/ce)[2]
    — y for i and i for y (e.g. arbitraryness)
    — s for z and z for s (e.g. Glazwegian)[2]
    — devoiced consonant for final voiced one (e.g. Laboff)
    — incorrect choice of C+ ion/ian/ial (e.g. paediatrition)
    — incorrect unstressed vowel (e.g. accessable, occurrance)
    — incorrect stressed vowel
        — changing pronunciation (e.g. adopted for adapted)
        — not changing pronunciation (e.g. speach)
    — incorrect plural/3rd sing/past tense (e.g. crys)
    — choice of wrong homophone (e.g. bare for bear, their for there)
    — misremembered words/names (e.g. Frankin & Redman)
    — realisation of assimilation (e.g. upmost *for* 'utmost')

— omissions:
    — single consonant for double
        — within morphemes (e.g. accomodate)
        — across morpheme boundaries (e.g. occured, occurence)
        — end of word (e.g. asses)
    — omission of vowel
        — silent (e.g. unhinderd)
        — not silent (e.g. socity)
    — omission of consonant
        — silent (e.g. condem)
        — not silent (e.g. prescibe)
    — omission of syllable(s) (e.g. expement)
    — omission of accent (e.g. Verdres)

— additions:
    — addition of vowel (e.g. arguement)
    — addition of consonant (not doubling) (e.g. Chompsky)
    — double consonant for single
        — within morphemes (e.g. accross)
        — across morpheme boundaries (e.g. innappropriate)
        — end of word (e.g. untill)
    — addition of syllable (e.g. uniformally)

— reversals/delays/anticipations:
    — reversal of vowel digraphs (e.g. recieve, acheive)
    — reversal of vowel and consonant (e.g. perscriptive)
    — reversal of separated vowels (e.g. relitavely)
    — reversal of consonants (e.g. ect.)
    — anticipation/delay (e.g. regconize)

— other:
    — likely typo or slip (e.g. lanjuage)
    — archaic attested spellings (e.g. Shakespere).

Of course there is no fail-safe way to differentiate between spelling errors and slips of the pen/typos (see for example Wing & Baddeley, 1980:254f), so, whilst 'fo' for 'of' was discarded as definitely a typing slip, instances in which there was any doubt at all have been included, though mostly categorised under 'other' as probable slips. The definition of a morpheme boundary can be difficult – it depends upon where you draw the line between active and/or transparent word formation on the one hand and etymology on the other (e.g. slopiness).

Distribution of spelling errors

Total number of words incorrectly spelt: 463; total number of errors within them: 493. Multiple occurrences of the same error by one person counted only once. The same error by the same person in derivational families (e.g. occured and occuring) counted only once.

Substitution	194	39%
Omission	159	32%
Addition	102	21%
Reversal, delay/anticipation	25	5%
Other	13	3%
Total	493	

Breakdown of substitution errors

unstressed vowel	124	64%
stressed vowel	8	4%
s for c and c for s	7	
y for i and i for y	3	7%
s for z and z for s	1	
devoiced C for voiced	2	
homophone	34	17.5%
C+ion,ian,ial etc.	5	2.5%
mis-spelt tense etc.	2	
misremembered word/name	6	5%
assimilation spelt	1	
other	1	
Total	194	

Most frequently mis-spelt words

(Number of times a word is spelt incorrectly by different people)

OCCURRENCE, OCCURRING etc.	17	WHERE as WERE	6
AITCHISON	15	ARGUMENT	4
SEPARATE etc.	11	(VOCAL) CORDS	4
PRONUNCIATION etc.	11	COMPLEMENT	4
ARBITRARY etc.	7	DEVELOPMENT, DEVELOPED	4
CONSCIOUS etc.	7	EXIST etc.	4
ACQUIRE, ACQUISITION etc.	6	INTEGRAL, INTEGRATE	4
DEPENDENT etc.	6	SENTENCE etc.	4
POSSESS etc.	6	AFFECT/EFFECT	4
THERE/THEIR	6	DEFINITE	3

GRAMMAR	3	RECEIVE	3
INTERRUPT etc.	3	TENDENCY	3
NECESSARY etc.	3	USAGE	3
PROFESSION etc.	3	WARDHAUGH	3
PSYCHO-	3	HOCKETT	3

Mis-spelt proper names:

In addition to those listed above, LABOV and CHOMSKY were each mis-spelt twice and 16 other proper names once each.

Double and single consonants

single for double:	within morpheme	17
	across morpheme boundary	31
	end of word	9
double for single:	within morpheme	17
	across morpheme boundary	10
	end of word	3

Discussion

It is impossible to disentangle patterns of errors from patterns and irregularities in English spelling. For example, the figures for double and single consonants at morpheme boundaries probably reflect an unequal original distribution. As Upward (1992) indicates, a strikingly large proportion of spelling errors in English do no more than lay bare the intricacies and illogicalities of the system, such that almost all errors would be eradicated under the implementation of a small number of conservative reforms (p. 92ff).

Word Boundaries

Our initial interest in word boundaries focussed on the writing of two words as one. Analysis indicated that this was not the whole story, however. In anticipation of differences of opinion, those examples below which strike us as likely to be contentious, are asterisked.

in(-)built and in(-)depth (14 people)

— as two words: 6
— hyphenated: 5
— as one word: 4 (one person wrote *in built* and *inbuilt)*

Other word-break types

hyphen used over word-break: 1

    Humans can pick-up when it is their turn to speak ...

hyphen used within single word: 8
>   *eight-teenth, inter-linked*, near-by, pre-conceptions, re-act, re-knowned (sic), sub-consciously, un-necessary*

hyphen omitted, leaving no gap: 5
>   *cooperate*, nonflexable (sic), nonprofessional, preset*, thirtysix*

two words written as one: 21

afterall	*infact (x3)*
alot (x5)	*inorder to*
anyway (deceive them in anyway)	*maybe (x3) (it maybe very difficult)*
aswell as	*middleclass**
eachother (x2)	*onto* (passed onto a receiver)
evermore (evermore important)	*someway (someway to explaining)*

hyphen omitted, leaving a space: 46

able bodied	*non standard (x2)*
age long	*non verbal**
child rearers	*over ambitious*
clear cut	*over polite*
cross links	*pin pointing*
deep seated	*purpose built*
ever debated	*re establish*
four legged	*rule governed* (x3)*
hyper creolization	*self critical*
ill thought of* (pre-nominal)	*self correction*
inter marriage	*self esteem*
lady like	*self learnt*
lip read (verb)	*semi permanent*
mentally handicapped* (pre-nominal)	*so called*
mid sentence	*stimulus bound*
no one	*structure dependent*
non instinctive	*sub varieties*
non fluent (x2)	*thirty six*
non native	*turn taking* (x3)*

one word written as two: 25

break down (the break down of)	*some what*
negotiations	*stereo types (x2)*
can not (x2)	*through out*
every day (in every day life)	*up date*

in to (x2) (research in to systems)	*what so ever*
logger heads	*when ever*
may be (May be if the thoughts…)	*where as (x5)*
meaning less	*where ever*
on going*	*world wide**
some where	

Discussion

Word-division is perhaps rather more fluid than other aspects of spelling, allowing individuals to adopt and defend their own preferences. This means that we have something of a moving target. The less confident individual might also be confused to find that, in some cases, the word-class determines which of two forms is used (e.g. mentally(-) handicapped); every( )day).

A Remedy?

Whilst prescriptivism asks who is to blame, who should pick up the pieces and whether writing skills matter, descriptivism – or pragmatism – might ask whether it isn't time for the mountain to move to Mohammed. The spelling system of English could be adjusted, such that the most troublesome features (reduced vowels, silent letters, doubled consonants, the apostrophe) simply disappear (Upward, 1992:92ff). Moves to spelling reform, however, have not been successful up to now.

Meanwhile, historical linguistics teaches us that, whilst the mountain may *think* it is staying where it is, a closer look at those successive cohorts of Mohammeds may reveal that they are not simply struggling towards it across the difficult terrain of English tradition, but shifting it, stone by stone, closer to some new location. Thus we may ask: what's going to happen next?

There was a time when *into, although* and *another* were all written as two words. Why should we be surprised to see other words go the same way? The genitive apostrophe is a relatively modern invention and errors have always been made in its use (Garrett & Austin, 1993). Perhaps it has had its day. For many centuries the spelling of words was open to negotiation. Are spellings not permitted to continue to change? The linguist can (just about) afford to take a 'watch and see what happens' approach.

Yet this is at odds with the conservatism of the educated and vocal general public. Those who believe that there has been a decline in standards as a direct result of liberal (non-prescriptive) education, and that it matters in some fundamental way, presumably welcome the new, stricter line laid down by the National Curriculum and expect it to rein in the wild horses.

The National Curriculum includes amongst the skills expected of pupils:

Key Stage 1 (age 5–7): being able to

- punctuate their writing, be consistent in their use of capital letters, full stops and question marks, and begin to use commas (DFE, 1995: 9)
- check the accuracy of their spelling (p. 10).

Key Stage 2 (age 7–11): being able to

- proofread – check the draft for spelling and punctuation errors, omissions or repetitions (p. 15)
- use punctuation marks correctly…, including full stops, question and exclamation marks, commas, inverted commas, and apostrophes to show possession (p. 15).

The methods for achieving these goals are, in principle at least, more enlightened than those of the past:

> National Curriculum English gives due weight to spelling, grammar and handwriting, but instead of the old boring exercises, young children are encouraged to write their own stories, to discuss them with the teacher and their friends, and to improve them, perhaps for printing in a class or school magazine. Grammar and knowledge about language can be introduced in their discussions with the teacher to help children improve their writing skills. (Cox, 1994: 29)

All the same, the underlying principle is prescriptive; but perhaps that is a red herring. Even voices that call for egalitarianism observe that:

> all children are entitled to be helped to use written and spoken standard English; this is the language of academic discourse, of national politics, of international usage. (Cox, 1994: 29)

Perhaps, as Marenbon (1994) argues, it is erroneous to juxtapose 'prescription' and 'description' in the first place, as if one could replace the other; each has its own purpose and indeed 'by describing how a certain language is spoken or written, the grammarian prescribes usage for those who wish to speak or write that language' (p. 20). But who gets to prescribe and who gets prescribed to? Have we got enough role-models left? Will our current, under-confident graduates be going into the classroom to describe and prescribe a variety they do not use themselves? Most importantly, are they, thanks to the reforms of the National Curriculum, the final cohort of progeny in a lost generation, or are they, perhaps, the spearhead of an escape from the conservatism of the over-educated few?

Notes

1 Tony Fairburn (personal communication) has pointed out that *alot* existed in the
   writing of those with limited education in the nineteenth century. It is, however, our
   impression that this spelling has not had a high profile in the writing of tertiary level
   students until very recently.
2 Where do spelling errors end and acceptable Americanisms begin? This is clearly a
   difficult category from this point of view.

References

Austin-Ward, B. (1986) English, English teaching and English teachers: The perceptions
   of 16 year olds. *Educational Research* 28(1), 32–42.
Cox, B. (1994) The National Curriculum in English. In S Brindley (ed.) *Teaching English.*
   Milton Keynes: Open University.
Department for Education (1995) *English in the National Curriculum.* London: HMSO.
Department of Education and Science (1975) *A Language for Life.* Report of the Com-
   mittee of Inquiry appointed by the Secretary of State for Education and Science under
   the chairmanship of Sir Alan Bullock, FBA. London: HMSO.
Garrett, P. and Austin, C. (1993) The English genitive apostrophe: Judgements of errors
   and implications for teaching. *Language Awareness* 2(2), 61–73.
Jeffs, A. (1985) *Children and Parents and Spelling.* Sheffield: Home and School Council
   Publications.
Marenbon, J. (1994) The new orthodoxy examined. In S. Brindley (ed.) *Teaching English.*
   Milton Keynes: Open University.
Peters, M. L. (1979) *Diagnostic and Remedial Spelling Manual* (revised edn). Basing-
   stoke: Macmillan.
Read, C. (1986) *Children's Creative Spelling.* London: Routledge & Kegan Paul.
Scottish Council for Research in Education (SCRE) (1961) *Studies in Spelling.* London:
   University of London Press.
Upward, C. (1992) Is traditionl english spelng mor dificlt than jermn? *Journal of Research
   in Reading* 15(2), 82–94.
Wing, A. M. and Baddeley, A. D. (1980) Spelling errors in handwriting: A corpus and a
   distributional analysis. In U. Frith (ed.) *Cognitive Processes in Spelling.* New York:
   Academic Press.

10 Knowing and Using the Perfect Tense in French

GEE MACRORY and VALERIE STONE
The Manchester Metropolitan University

Introduction

To many Modern Foreign Languages (MFLs) teachers, research into second language acquisition may seem remote from their everyday concerns. The debate as to how second or foreign languages are acquired may appear to be a theoretical one. Moreover, given the relative amounts of research undertaken in English language teaching (ELT) contexts and MFLs ones, they could be forgiven for thinking that this debate was one which had little to say to them. Yet, as Ellis states:

> Every time teachers make a pedagogic decision about content or methodology, they are, in fact, making assumptions about how learners learn. The study of SLA may help teachers in two ways. First, it will enable them to make their assumptions explicit, so that they can examine them critically. In this way, it will help them to develop their own explicit ideas of how the kind of learners they are teaching acquire an L2. Second, it will provide them information that they can use when they make future pedagogic decisions. (1994: 4)

This, of course, is no less true of MFLs teachers than it is of teachers of ELT. And for both MFLs and ELT teachers, the extent to which their assumptions are made explicit, as well as the extent to which their actions are consciously affected by them, is, at least in part, inhibited by external factors. Those external factors, however, will vary according to time and place. For MFLs teachers, for example, the nature and extent of recent changes (notably, GCSE and the National Curriculum) may have made them less able to concentrate on how learners learn, as they have necessarily grappled with changes at the level of both content and methodology. In particular, a focus on teaching language for the purposes of communication (with all that that implies), the use of authentic materials to teach both spoken and written language, as well as a requirement to maximise the use of the target language in the classroom are changes, albeit positive, which can conspire to emphasise teaching at the expense of learning. *What* is to be taught and *how* it is to be taught are issues of major concern to the majority of classroom teachers. They are also reassuringly visible, tangible therefore in a way in which language learning is not. This is not to imply that teachers lack concern as to what happens inside their learners' heads. On the contrary, our recent experience of teachers' forums suggests that they are keen to move beyond the practicalities of the everyday classroom. Rather, it is to highlight the everyday pressures that can militate against the reflective stance that so many teachers of MFLs would wish to take.

Teaching, Learning and Grammar

Of all the things that have to be taught and learned in the language classroom, perhaps one of the most enduring concerns for teachers is the vexed question of grammar. Pica (1994: 51) lists ten questions frequently asked by teachers, several of which reflect a concern with structure and accuracy, and one of which is 'How much attention should be given to explicit grammar instruction?' If MFLs teachers have difficulty in answering this question, this is perhaps not very surprising. The report of the National Curriculum (NC) working party comments (DES/WO, 1990: 57) that 'modern language teaching and learning has suffered in the past from extremes of practice and nowhere more than in the treatment of grammar'. The report itself, however, along with a range of GCSE syllabuses, is criticised by Mitchell (1994a) for failing to offer clear guidance to teachers. She describes the advice available to MFLs teachers as characterised by a lack of clarity and consistency, particularly in two areas, namely the kind of grammatical models most relevant to pedagogy and the relationship between grammar study and language learning (1994b: 215). It is this latter area that we propose to consider in more detail.

Knowledge of Language and Ability to Use

Although the move towards communicative language teaching tended to play down the value of grammar teaching (Tonkyn, 1994: 4), teachers themselves, according to Green & Hecht (1992: 168), appear to have lost none of their faith in it. Mitchell & Hooper (1992: 47) found that the MFLs teachers they interviewed 'generally believed that a clear positive relationship existed between explicit knowledge about language and the development of practical language proficiency'. How they provide learners with that explicit knowledge may, of course, have changed over the years. Mitchell (1994b: 216–7) reports a tendency towards the inductive teaching of grammatical structures, in that the teachers in her study reported that any discussion of grammar followed rather than preceded the presentation and practice of new structures. The perceived relationship between language knowledge and language proficiency is not, then, solely the province of teachers who adhere to a more traditional and deductive method of language teaching. Indeed, Cross (1995: 84) claims that what he describes as two opposing methodology camps, that is, proponents of inductive and deductive teaching methods, have in common the view that learning is facilitated by knowing rules.

We may justifiably ask, then, if research into SLA bears out the contention that explicit knowledge of the target language is related to the ability to use it. It is important to note that there are very different perspectives on this. One perspective, which is heavily influenced not only by research findings from naturalistic contexts for SLA, but also by research into first language acquisition, allows little, if any room, for formal instruction (Krashen, 1982; Dulay, Burt & Krashen, 1982), and accords priority to learner internal mechanisms. Unconscious processes guide the learner in acquiring the language from the input, in a developmental sequence common to all learners of the language as a first language, and the provision of appropriate learning experiences should suffice. Formal instruction is neither necessary nor helpful. However, this is not a view that currently attracts broad support. Firstly, it could be said to draw rather simplistically upon research into first language acquisition, and, secondly, it does not acknowledge sufficiently the range of contexts in which second languages are learned. While the increased emphasis on authentic input and opportunities for interaction within the classroom has brought rewards, as Pica (1994: 65) points out, 'for many learners, especially those for whom the classroom is a sole context for language learning, meaningful interaction and comprehensible input may not be possible … This situation suggests that learners may need a more efficient means to access the grammar rules of the language they are trying to learn than through input provision and interactional experiences alone'. Although this may well strike a chord with many classroom teachers and indeed learners, research findings are by no means clear cut. It is not our intention here to review the numerous studies that have attempted to resolve this issue, as this is more than adequately done elsewhere (see, for example, Long, 1983; Ellis, 1990; Larsen-Freeman & Long, 1991; Lightbown & Spada, 1993; Nunan, 1995). Although there are a number of studies which suggest that formal instruction has little effect (see, for example, Ellis, 1984), a number of variables make interpretation of the research findings less than straightforward. Variation in the learning contexts, duration of instruction, the way in which 'instruction' as a term is understood and how 'effects' are measured are only some of the factors that make this a complex area to investigate. Attempts to control for some of these variables have yielded interesting results. For example, Pica (1985) compared the effects of instruction upon classroom learners of English and learners acquiring English outside the classroom. This study found that classroom instruction had a distinct but selective impact upon production, proving more useful for linguistically simple forms than for complex ones. Moreover, for aspects of the grammar which proved resistant to instruction, Pica found similar production patterns between the learners who had received no formal instruction and the classroom learners.

Studies such as the above are useful in that they may help us to reconcile evidence for developmental sequences with evidence for the effects of formal instruction. While formal instruction has generally been understood to refer to grammar teaching (Ellis, 1994: 611), the *effects* of such instruction, of course, may or may not include explicit knowledge of the rule system. While Ellis (1994: 659) concludes that 'the case for formal instruction is strengthening', he notes also that 'it is not yet clear which kind of instruction works best ... There may also be a case for consciousness raising directed at helping learners to formulate explicit knowledge'.

This brings us back to the link between explicit knowledge and performance, in which it would appear that many teachers still place their trust. Appearing to confirm this, Green & Hecht (1992) found in their study of 300 German pupils learning English, that when they were able to state a correct rule, they performed considerably better than when they could give only an incorrect rule (1992: 179). However, they found that their results did not apply uniformly to all twelve of the rules they investigated, prompting them to note that the solution may be in identifying what is hard to learn and what is easy to learn. This is of course consistent with the results of the study by Pica (1985) and would also appear to lend support to her suggestion that some areas of the target grammar be excluded from direct presentation. As yet, however, we are still unclear as to precisely which parts of the grammatical system are more amenable to intervention. Given also that we do not know enough about how immediate or durable the effects of instruction are, it would be premature to start rewriting syllabuses. This is particularly true of languages other than English, and we would support wholeheartedly the research agenda put forward by Mitchell (1994b: 220), who notes the continuing need for research into links between explicit knowledge of target language systems and the state of learners' procedural competence, that is, their ability to make use of that knowledge.

The Purpose of the Present Study

From our discussions with teachers and the trainee teachers on our Postgraduate Certificate in Education (PGCE) course, it would appear that, despite a recent tendency to teach some grammatical structures as unanalysed lexical items, it is common for certain grammar rules to be taught explicitly, that is, for the rules of formation and use to be specified – a situation consistent with Mitchell's findings. It is by no means clear, however, to what extent learners' own claims about their knowledge of rules are related to their ability to apply them in practice exercises, nor whether either of these enables them to make use of particular structures in communicative tasks. Ellis has emphasised the value of SLA research to teachers (see introduction to this paper), but it is frequently the case that teachers themselves view research as extremely remote from the reality of their work in the classroom (Green & Hecht, 1992). Thus, we aimed to collect data that was readily available to teachers themselves, and also to do so in a way that teachers would find easy to replicate. We decided, therefore, to concentrate on a small number of pupils in one teacher's classroom, and to look in some detail at learners' knowledge and use of a commonly taught grammatical structure.

As pointed out above, discussions with teachers and trainees suggest that contemporary practice includes some explicit treatment of grammatical structures. This includes, in particular, the perfect tense. However, it is worth giving brief consideration to the way in which this relates to other means of expressing past time in French. The perfect tense corresponds essentially to the simple past or to the present perfect in English, and contrasts with the imperfect tense, which is used to express not only the past but also past progressive and past habitual action. The important distinction is one of aspect rather than of time. Kaplan (1987) summarises this as 'marking what might generally be referred to as the discreteness of an action versus state of being, or what is also termed an event versus non-event distinction' (1987: 52). Hence the tense used to render durative verbs such as *aimer, pouvoir, vouloir* in the past tends to be the imperfect rather than the perfect.

The acquisition of this distinction has been the subject of a number of studies (see, for example, Kaplan, 1987; Bergstrom, 1994), and we recognise the importance of learners acquiring this distinction in order to have a working tense system in French. However, it appears to be the case that this distinction is acquired only slowly, with the perfect tense being acquired, generally speaking, before the imperfect (Kaplan, 1987; Harley, 1992). Kaplan suggests that one possible reason for this could be a tendency on the part of teachers to regard the perfect tense as a more reliable means of eliciting conversation about the past as it can prompt a list of events. The possibility, therefore, that the perfect tense was likely to be acquired first, and to be prioritised in the classroom, suggested both that this might be a more fruitful avenue for investigating the relationship between knowledge and use, and that it might also seem more closely connected to the reality of classroom work for many teachers. That reality includes the possibility that, for a number of reasons, many learners may not acquire the perfect/imperfect distinction within the time span during which they are required to study a Modern Foreign Language.

The Procedure

Ten pupils were selected from the middle range of ability in a Year 10 French group. The study focused on a comparison between:

- learners' own perceptions of what they knew about forming and using the perfect tense
- their actual knowledge of a variety of forms within the perfect tense
- their ability to use the structure in speaking and in writing.

In the first stage, in order to establish pupils' own perceptions of what they knew about the perfect tense, they were asked to state anything they knew about forming and using it, and their comments were recorded and transcribed verbatim. They were told that they could say as much or as little as they wanted, and they were reassured that it was not a test and had no implications for their class assessment.

A production task was chosen to assess learners' knowledge, as we wanted to establish what language the learners might have (potentially) at their disposal. A gap-filling exercise was devised to assess pupils' knowledge of the perfect tense, taking account of those aspects of the structure which had been presented in the course book, namely all persons of the two auxiliaries, the three regular forms of the past participle, a range of irregular past participles, and past participle agreement with *être* as the auxiliary. The format chosen was 32 unconnected sentences, with the infinitive given in brackets at the end of the sentence, as this was an exercise already familiar to the pupils. For the oral part of the exercise, they were asked what the forms of the missing items were and their answers were recorded; for the written version, they were asked to complete the same sentence in writing. Both spoken and written production were elicited to guard against the possibility that a written version alone might have included what were in fact spelling mistakes, particularly given the number of available spellings for the vowel /e/ in French. A spoken version alone would have been a most unfamiliar task. In addition, it allowed for an analysis of the relationship between spoken and written language at a later date.

Learners' ability to make use of their knowledge was assessed through a semi-structured interview on the topic of the family's previous summer holiday. They were not instructed to use the perfect tense, but all interviews began with the same question: 'L'année dernière, pendant les grandes vacances, qu'est-ce que tu as fait?'. Whilst questions were explicitly formulated with the specific purpose of encouraging learners to use a variety of forms and verbs, open questions were included to offer them opportunities to respond without the influence of the questioner. Interviews lasted approximately five minutes.

Although pupils were asked about themselves and their own activities, each was also asked questions which enabled them to talk about one other person and also about a number of other people, so that in addition to first person singular forms, we were also able to elicit third person singular and plural forms. After some common opening questions, most questions arose from what the pupils themselves said. The written account was based on the same holiday, and instructions were given in English. Pupils took approximately ten minutes to complete it, although no actual limit was set.

Results: Knowledge

Pupils' perceptions

Most pupils were clear that *être* and *avoir* were important components in forming the Perfect Tense, although there was some confusion between *avoir* and *aller,* and one pupil specified that *être* would be used in conjunction with 'going' words. There was substantial agreement that the past participle was recognisable by its final accent. A few specified *é,* but the pupil who gave other details reversed the *i* and *u* endings of *ir* and *re* verbs. There were some residual memories of agreement based on gender, and exemplification of this led to comments such as:

> 'the second part of the verb, you have to put an accent over the e and you add e if it's feminine'.

All commented on the need to use the perfect tense to talk about past actions and there were references to 'what you did', 'what you've done', 'what you did last week/yesterday'. One pupil attempted to be more specific about the kind of situation which might determine the use of the structure, suggesting 'when you write a letter', and into the realm of imagination and creativity, 'when you speak to someone who is upper class'! There was no reference to the perfect/imperfect distinction, but it is likely that this simply reflects the fact that the pupils had had exposure only to the perfect tense at this stage. Indeed, this is consistent with Kaplan's (1987) suggestion, noted above, that teachers prioritise the perfect tense.

Clearly, pupils could recall some aspects of the rules which they had been taught. They were most sure about the need for an auxiliary and about the use of the perfect tense to describe past events, but other details were forgotten, hazy or confused.

Gap-filling tests

On a simple marking scheme, awarding a point each for the correct spoken form of the auxiliary verb and the past participle, seven out of ten pupils scored over 50% accuracy. Analysis of the data shows a degree of individual variation, including the sole use of *avoir* as auxiliary, the non-systematic alternation of *avoir, être* and *aller,* and the variability of auxiliary within the same verb, notably with *aller, rester* and *arriver.*

However, out of the ten pupils eight offered both an auxiliary and a past participle on every occasion, and a ninth pupil did so on some occasions and not on others, reflecting the views already expressed when asked for their perceptions. This consistency was apparent also in the case of the pupil who consistently omitted the auxiliary, as her account of her own knowledge was by far the vaguest. This was in contrast to the generally high degree of consistency in the successful production of regular past participles, although there were many errors in the production of the irregular past participles.

The written test imposed greater demands upon the pupils, such as appropriate past participle agreement, and therefore the overall scores were lower than for the oral test. However, analysis of the written data reveals that individual pupils' knowledge was relatively consistent across the spoken and written versions. For example, the same pupils omitted the auxiliary, made sole use of *avoir,* used *aller* as an alternative auxiliary, and to a lesser extent than in the oral exercise, varied the auxiliary within the same verb, notably with *rester.* Similar difficulties were encountered with irregular past participles. There seemed to be some awareness that, in the written form, in some cases the past participle needed to agree with the subject, but correct use was variable and it sometimes occurred in spite of an incorrect choice of auxiliary, producing, for example, *elle a retournée.*

Again, the consistent offering of an auxiliary reflected the views expressed by the pupils. It would appear that despite the fact that the highest score was 58%, what the pupils did know was that an auxiliary verb was needed. Furthermore, a separate analysis of each pupil's performance revealed a generally high degree of accuracy with the auxiliary in terms of person and number, suggesting that what the pupils were unsure about was which auxiliary verb to use. Once that choice was made, it was likely to be correct in person and number.

Results: Use

As stated above, pupils were asked in an oral interview how they had spent their summer holidays during the previous year. They were also asked to give a written account.

In the oral interviews we took care to ensure that the initial question had been understood to refer to past time through the use of gesture or paraphrase. Nevertheless, on some occasions pupils reverted to the present tense, despite the consistency of their stated perceptions that the perfect tense is used to describe past events. Where the perfect tense was used, it was mainly in the first person singular where pupils seemed to be relatively confident. From 87 examples of the first person singular, 50 contained both an auxiliary and a past participle. However, when pupils were given opportunities to speak about other members of the family or friends, on only five out of 30 occasions did they include an auxiliary, and in all cases the form was incorrect. This was a pattern replicated in the written account. Again, a tendency to revert to the present tense was evident, but where the perfect tense was used, there was an even stronger tendency to use the first person singular. From 56 examples of this, 32 included both an auxiliary and a past participle, whereas from 32 examples containing a third person singular or plural pronoun, only six contained any auxiliary.

In both the oral and written versions, the lexical verbs offered were limited to a small number of regular verbs such as *jouer, nager, regarder, visiter* and *voyager,* where, for the most part, pupils offered the correct past participle. There was little attempt to make use of irregular verbs.

Discussion

Questioning pupils about their perceptions suggested very strongly that they knew that *avoir* or *être* was needed to form the perfect tense. This knowledge was partially demonstrated in the gap-filling activities, in that in the vast majority of answers an auxiliary verb was supplied, even if this was *aller,* which is used as an auxiliary in the formation of the future. Furthermore, they also displayed the ability to select the correct form of their chosen auxiliary in terms of person and number. The data suggest, therefore, that for most of the pupils, there was at least the beginning of some knowledge about this area of the target grammar. However, the tendency to omit the auxiliary when speaking or writing the perfect tense, and the marked difference between the first and third persons of the verb, raise a number of interesting questions. At first sight it may be tempting to draw the conclusion that the pupils have knowledge that they are not making use of. But, although the pupils clearly had some developing knowledge of this area of the grammar, what is less clear is the extent to which they were sure the answers in the gap-filling tests were in fact correct. Green & Hecht (1992) suggest that it is knowledge of *correct* rules that may be facilitative to performance. This raises the question of how secure knowledge has to be before it can be brought into use.

One obvious possibility is that the focus on the message rather than the form is responsible for the disparity between performance on the gap-filling and the conversation task. This could be because of processing constraints, or because of a perceived lack of importance of accuracy in the message- focused activities. The latter would not account for the difference between the use of auxiliaries with first and with third person, and while the former suggestion, namely the effect of processing constraints, might do so, another possibility is that the first person utterances have been heavily practised in class and are functioning as unanalysed routines. That there were some examples of the type *ma mère j'ai joué* would offer tentative support for this possibility. It may well be that a combination of processing constraints and an insecure knowledge of the rules means that the most readily available information is via routines practised extensively in class.

What then are the implications for the classroom? Clearly, any conclusions from a small scale study are necessarily tentative. Nevertheless, a number of points can be usefully considered. The first of these is the question of the role that routines might play in language learning, and the implications of this for classroom-based input. If, at least in the short term, they provide a means whereby learners can engage in communication, they serve a purpose. The contribution that they might make to language acquisition in the longer term is rather more controversial (for a recent overview, see Weinert, 1995). What is evident is that however useful they might be, they cannot be the sole source of input in a classroom. Learners cannot practise every person of the perfect tense in this way; the question for classroom teachers, therefore, is how other parts of the target grammar, in this case the perfect tense, are provided for the learners so that reliance on routines gives way to control over a more complete rule system. There are implications here for the use of, for example, texts which refer to third parties so that pupils have access to other parts of the rule system of the perfect tense.

A further consideration for the classroom is that the information gained from gap-filling or other tests to see whether pupils have 'learned' specific grammatical structures is limited in its usefulness, and needs to be supplemented by information gathered about the pupils' ability to use language. It follows from this that learners may need more meaning-focused activities to use the language they have been provided with, be that routines or grammatical rules. In the first instance, a review of the balance of such activities could be a positive move forward.

Acknowledgements

We would like to thank Cheadle Hulme High School, Stockport, for their willingness to participate in this project. We are particularly grateful to the Year 10 pupils involved, and to their class teacher, Carolyn Lofkin.

References

Bergstrom, A. (1994) The expression of temporal reference by learners of French: Report on the narratives. Paper presented to AAAL Conference, Baltimore, March 1994.

Cross, D. (1995) Formal instruction in language teaching programmes. *Language Learning Journal* 9, 82–4.

DES/WO (1990) *Modern Foreign Languages in the National Curriculum*. London: Department of Education and Science & Welsh Office.

Dulay, H., Burt, M. and Krashen, S. (1982) *Language Two*. Oxford: Oxford University Press.

Ellis, R. (1984) Can syntax be taught? A study of the effects of formal instruction on the acquisition of WH questions by children. *Applied Linguistics* 5(2), 138–55.

— (1990) *Instructed Second Language Acquisition*. Oxford: Blackwell.

— (1994) *The Study of Second Language Acquisition*. Oxford: Oxford University Press.

Green, P. S. and Hecht, K. (1992) Implicit and explicit grammar: An empirical study. *Applied Linguistics* 13(2), 168–84.

Harley, B. (1992) Patterns of second language development in French immersion. *French Language Studies* 2, 159–83.

Kaplan, M. A. (1987) Developmental patterns of past tense acquisition among foreign language learners of French. In B. Van Patten, T. R. Dvorak and J. F. Lee (eds) *Foreign Language Learning: A Research Perspective*. Rowley, MA: Newbury House.

Krashen, S. (1982) *Principles and Practice in Second Language Acquisition*. Oxford: Pergamon.

Larsen-Freeman, D. and Long, M. H. (1991) *An Introduction to Second Language Acquisition Research*. Harlow: Longman.

Lightbown, P. and Spada, N. (1993) *How Languages are Learned*. Oxford: Oxford University Press.

Long, M. (1983) Does second language instruction make a difference? A review of the research. *TESOL Quarterly* 17, 359–82.

Mitchell R. (1994a) Grammar, syllabuses and teachers. In M. Bygate, A. Tonkyn and E. Williams (eds) *Grammar and the Language Teacher*. London: Prentice Hall International.

— (1994b) Foreign language teachers and the teaching of grammar. In M. Bygate, A. Tonkyn and E. Williams (eds) *Grammar and the Language Teacher*. London: Prentice Hall International.

Mitchell, R. and Hooper, J. (1992) Teachers' views of language knowledge. In C. James and P. Garrett (eds) *Language Awareness in the Classroom*. London: Longman.

Nunan, D. (1995) Closing the gap between learning and instruction. *TESOL Quarterly* 29(1), 133–59.

Pica, T. (1985) The selective impact of classroom instruction on second-language acquisition. *Applied Linguistics* 6(3), 215–22.

— (1994) Questions from the language classroom: Research perspectives. *TESOL Quarterly* 28(1), 49–79.

Tonkyn, A. (1994) Introduction: Grammar and the language teacher. In M. Bygate, A. Tonkyn and E. Williams (eds) *Grammar and the Language Teacher*. London: Prentice Hall International.

Weinert, R. (1995) The role of formulaic language in second language acquisition: A review. *Applied Linguistics* 16(2), 180–205.

Notes on Contributors

Thomas Bloor has taught EFL, linguistics and applied linguistics and worked in language education administration and teacher education in the UK, Ethiopia and Botswana, with short stints in many other countries. He currently teaches linguistics and discourse analysis to TEFL/TESP master's students at Aston University. He is co-author with Meriel Bloor of *The Functional Analysis of English* (Arnold). Research interests are EAP, discourse analysis, grammar and language in education.

George Blue works in the Language Centre and the Centre for Language in Education at the University of Southampton. He teaches and coordinates EAP courses for international students as well as teaching on postgraduate courses in applied linguistics. He is currently Chair of the Institute for English Language Teacher Development in Higher Education. His research interests include language in education, EAP and learner autonomy.

Christopher Brumfit is Professor of Education and Director of the Centre for Language at the University of Southampton. He has degrees in literature, applied linguistics and education, and has worked substantially in Tanzania and the UK, with lengthy working visits to China, India, and Canada. He was Chair of BAAL from 1982–5, then a Vice-President of AILA, and has published more than 30 books on language and literature in education.

A. P. Cowie is Reader in Lexicography in the School of English at Leeds University. He has written widely on the theory and practice of dictionary-making, on the vocabulary of English (especially its phraseology) and the learning and teaching of vocabulary. He is chief editor of the *Oxford Advanced Learner's Dictionary*, fourth edition, and co-author of the *Oxford Dictionary of Current Idiomatic English.*

Alan Davies was a member of staff of the Department of Applied Linguistics at the University of Edinburgh from 1965 to 1995. He is now Emeritus Professor there and a Professorial Fellow at the University of Melbourne, where he is attached to the Language Testing Research Centre. He is a former editor of *Applied Linguistics* and of *Language Testing* and author of *Principles of Language Testing* (Blackwell, 1990) and *The Native Speaker in Applied Linguistics* (Edinburgh University Press, 1991).

Simon Gieve has taught EFL in Thailand and Japan. Since 1992 he has been registered as a PhD student in the Department of Linguistics at Lancaster University, where he has also found occasional part-time work teaching academic study skills, on MA courses in applied linguistics, and in EFL teacher training. His interests are in critical discourse analysis, academic writing, teacher education and classroom research.

Peter Howarth has worked in the English Language Unit at Leeds University for the last ten years. He teaches postgraduate courses in applied linguistics and language teaching methodology as well as a variety of EAP and ESP courses for teachers and other professionals. His chief area of research is phraseology, in particular the native and non-native use of collocations in academic writing.

James P. Lantolf has been a Professor of Applied Linguistics at Cornell University since 1991. He has also been on the faculty of the University of Delaware, the University of Texas at San Antonio and the State University of New York at Geneseo. He is co-editor of *Applied Linguistics*. His areas of interest include sociocultural theory, metaphor in second language learning and the effects of learning a second language on cognition. His current project focuses on understanding the interface between the experimental laboratory and the second language classroom.

Gee Macrory has taught Modern Foreign Languages (MFLs) in further education and in secondary schools. She has been an LEA advisory teacher, and since 1990 has been a teacher trainer at the Didsbury School of Education, Manchester Metropolitan University. Her interests include the role of grammar in language learning, early bilingual language acquisition and the education of pupils for whom English is an additional language.

Neil Mercer is Reader and Director of the Centre for Language and Communications at the Open University, Milton Keynes. His research has mainly been on language use and the process of teaching and learning, in schools and other settings. He wrote *Common Knowledge: The development of understanding in the classroom* (Methuen/Routledge, 1987) with Derek Edwards, and his most recent book is *The Guilded Construction of Knowledge: Talk amongst teachers and learners* (Multilingual Matters, 1995).

Rosamond Mitchell is a Reader in Education, and Chair of the Centre for Language in Education, at the University of Southampton. She teaches postgraduate courses in applied linguistics and educational research methods; her research interests include classroom based language learning and language education policy. She is a former editor of *Applied Linguistics*, and the current Chair of the British Association for Applied Linguistics (BAAL).

Valerie Stone has taught Modern Foreign Languages (MFLs) in secondary schools and in Higher Education. Since 1982 she has been a teacher trainer at the

Didsbury School of Education, Manchester Metropolitan University. Her interests include the role of grammar in language learning and MFLs in initial teacher education. She was a member of the National Curriculum Working Party for MFLs, and has been a governor of the Centre for Information on Language Teaching and Research (CILT).

Wondwosen Tamrat has taught EFL at all levels of the Ethiopian education system and is currently employed as a lecturer in English at Kotobe College of Teacher Education near Addis Ababa. He has a BA in English Language and Literature from Addis Ababa University and postgraduate degrees from Addis Ababa and Warwick Universities. His research interests include curriculum design and evaluation.

Alison Wray is Assistant Director of the Wales Applied Language Research Unit at the University of Wales Swansea. Until 1996 she was a Senior Lecturer in Linguistics at the University College of Ripon and York St John. Besides her interests in student writing, she has published research in psycholinguistics and in the reconstruction of the pronunciation of English, French and Latin for singers of Early Music.